THE HIDDEN TRUTH

Dr. Bishop Dambar Adhikari

INDIA • SINGAPORE • MALAYSIA

ISBN 979-8-88959-624-0

Contents

Introduction of The Author

Dr. Bishop Dambar Adhikari was born as the first child in an ordinary family in 1962 in Okhaldhunga district of Eastern Nepal, Province No. 1 (Mount Everest region). Bishop Adhikari came to Kathmandu at the age of 16 and continued his studies. He lived a struggling life, doing various businesses. During that time, he used to spend time with various experts while looking for the history of his native land from bookshops and also spending time with various experts to satisfy his taste.

At the same time, he left Nepal in 1987 and went to Bahrain to work. A year after arriving there, he went to Egypt from Bahrain. After one year, he returned to Bahrain again and from there, he went to America to do theology as planned by the Operation Mobilization Organization. During the transit in Germany, according to God's will, he was ordained as a pastor at the American Army Baptist Church in Germany and completed five years of service. Then, he started the Bringing the Gospel back to Europe campaign. He has reached 30 countries and delivered good news to the people of 125 countries along with various other services. Now, he lives in Germany along with his wife, two sons and one daughter. His whole family is working in ministry. Along with his wife, Bishop Dambar Adhikari has been providing counselling among students and pastors in various Bible colleges.

Although he went to different places during his ministry, he did not stop researching his interests. "Remember the days of old, Consider the years of many generations. Ask your father, and he will show you; your elders, and they will tell you." Meditating on Deuteronomy 32:7, he travelled to many countries and learned many languages, studied the roots of that language as well as other festivals and customs, instruments and lifestyles.

According to the same study, by researching the lifestyles and customs of not only Nepal but also India and other places, this book has revealed the truth that the festivals and instruments that are being celebrated as our Nepali cultural practices as our identity are not Nepal's but originated from outside and came to Nepal in this book. Also, in order to bring the history of Nepal and Nepalese into the hands of the readers, the true facts, history, and history have been explained in easily in this book.

Education

☐ From 1990 to 1992 General Biblical Course

☐ One-year European Theology Research Seminary

☐ Two years Biblical Counselling

☐ Three years Presbyterian and Anglican B.Th.

☐ Master of Pastoral Counselling

Responsibility and Ministry Identity

1. Director of the IMF International Missionary Fellowship Church Planting Project in Multicultural society.

2. Associate director of Logos Bible College, India, Hyderabad

3. Co-worker of Kontack Mission Church Planting Project in Multicultural society

4. Pastor of ICC International Christ Center in Wanne Eickel Multicultural society in Germany

Congratulations

I am very grateful for the opportunity to write the foreword of the book written by Bishop Dr. Dambar Adhikari.

While looking at the manuscript, I found Dr. Dambar put his heart, compassion and hard work of research into completing this book.

Deeply researched, this book can be called a unique book. I am confident that this book will play an important role in understanding the history of the Nepalese clan and its beginnings. The author has highlighted historical facts to prove the issues raised by him. This book will help students of the Bible and historians.

I am thankful to Dr. Dambar for bringing this book to the Nepali world. This book is a must read for every believer. I have been so blessed to read this book. It actually creates a sense of curiosity and learning when one starts reading the book. The Nepali Christian world will be proud to have God's servant Dambar Adhikari.

I have known him for more than a decade. I found him courageous, inspiring, humble, visionary, committed, dedicated, and friendly. He is reaching out to the wider Nepali community. I wish his book continued success and hope to read his other books.

– Rev. Dr. Hem Sagar Rasaily

Director, Logos Bible College

Principal, Logos Theological Seminary

Senior Pastor, Living Word Church, Hyderabad, India •

Vice-Chancellor, Shalom Vision Bible College, Malaysia

General Secretary, Nations Association for Theological Accreditation (NATA), India

 This important book is the product of historical investigative study written by Bishop Dr. Dambar Adhikari and is beneficial and educationally useful for all those who are interested in history, culture, anthropology and biblical events. This is a book that we Nepali Christians should study deeply and learn many relevant things from.

There is no doubt that writings based on factual truth will be a new dimension in the world of literature, culture and history. If this book is accepted as a part of the curriculum by the relevant schools and universities for the study of religion, history, culture and anthropology, we can be sure that all the learners will get more benefits. This is a book that everyone must read once. Hoping to read more such research papers from the author, I express my gratitude to the respected author. Congratulations and best wishes.

Thank you.

– J.V. Shah.
M.B.B.S., M.B.E.H., Graduate (Naturopathic Medicine).
Active political worker (Nepali political party "National Liberation Movement" The Central Governor of Nepal).

I had the opportunity to receive and read some parts of the book called *The Hidden Truth* written by Bishop Dr. Dambar Adhikari based on his experiences and knowledge gained abroad with many prayers. He has visited 30 different countries of the world.

In this book, he has revealed the history of the lineages of all four communities and compared the truth of the Bible with I have full confidence that this important book written by him with a lot of effort will give the readers an opportunity to know about it and I want to inspire everyone to read this book.

I would like to express my gratitude and thanks to the author of this book, Bishop Dr. Dambar Adhikari.

I would like to congratulate the writer with a prayer that God fulfils his intentions.

– Rev. Philemon Khadka Chhetri, D. D
International Director, New Life Mission

I had the opportunity to read an interesting and research-based book. I am assured the author, Bishop Dr. Dambar Adhikari has prepared a solid material after much historical studies and research. The book is suitable for a deeper historical study. Therefore, this is a source text.

Author Dr. Bishop Dambar has offered answers to many unanswered questions among the common Nepalese, again in an accessible style of writing, with proper historical references. This is the first book of its kind that dealt with the rise and dispersal of the tribes and communities based on their trades and professions. Referencing the Old Testament, the history and traditions of the Jewish people have been traced down and illustrated as to how they are similar to Nepalese civilization and traditions.

The colourful illustrations and pictures in the book have rendered the contents even more meaningful and interesting. The size, cover design, and letter fonts make the book easy to read and comfort the eyes. I hope to see more such research-based books from the author, and it's my prayer that many will be enlightened and informed by the book!

– Dr. Bishop Narayan Sharma
Believers Eastern Church,
Jorhat, Assam, India

Preface

A teaching that has confused the people living in the neighbouring countries of India and Nepal for centuries is that when asked about human creation, it can be read in various articles that Brahma created five types of people. Since childhood, I used to ask teachers and various people about the fact that there were very few people who raised questions about this creation and were forced to accept that teaching. Can it not be denied because the creator Brahma created it in this way? I was often bothered by this question. Why was I born? Who created me? Who is holding the earth? What will happen after my death? Creator Brahma created Brahmins, Kshatriyas, Vaishyas, Shudras, and Dalits, but who created women? The question began to arise in me. Of course, there is some error in it or it is not well explained. I got the trick and, of course, the curiosity to find out something about it increased. I started to feel that I was responsible for it.

After that, while searching and researching books and articles related to various history, religious laws, instruments with festivals, etc., I found evidence that the religious laws, instruments with festivals, and various symbols that are popular in Nepal are not original to Nepal but come from somewhere else. Many years of study and research to confirm this evidence inspired me to write this book. I had the opportunity to visit and research in 30 countries of the world, including European countries. Apart from Nepal and India, there is a class system in other countries. Of course, this class system has not been affected in Europe. But even though the Lord Jesus was born in Asia and Christianity also started from Asia, it is well known that those who believed in Jesus Christ were exiled in Asia, especially in Nepal and India.

In Europe, the gospel of Jesus reached later than in Asia, but they quickly believed in Jesus and accepted it, and it is found that human consciousness developed. After that, the class system existing in Europe came to an end soon. Today, the same Europeans and Americans came with various projects in the Asian continent including Nepal and India to show God's love. In India and Nepal, those missionaries were accused of bringing European religion, but the truth is that the origin of Christianity is Asia. More and more Nepalese and Indians have gone to Europe and America. In Nepal and India, everything that came from outside is said to be ours, but Christianity is said to be someone else's, but everything in Nepal and India came from outside. So much so that it has been proved here that the aboriginals, Mongols, Untouchables, Shah Dynasty, and Aryans who are living here have also come here from outside.

The purpose of this book is to show that we are all children of the same Creator God. God created us as male and female. Understanding this truth is necessary for us to live together and eliminate the caste discrimination that exists among Nepalese and speed up the development of the nation.

Acknowledgments

First of all, I thank my Lord because just as He gave Moses the call and burden to say, "Let my people go, so that they may worship me." He also gave me the same call, vision, and burden. Because, without Jesus, no people are worthy to worship God. He freed those who were enmeshed in different customs and different backgrounds and communities from slavery. According to the same call, I got the opportunity to travel to different countries and abroad. Our background and our descendants were found outside Nepal. May this revelation be given to the entire readership through this hidden truth book to come out of their background to worship our true Lord God and to do the same to others.

I would like to thank my wife, Barbara, for not only her prayers and her time but also her great contribution in writing this book. In addition, my sons and daughters have encouraged me and financially supported me along with prayers. And my spiritual loved ones have also helped me a lot.

I am especially grateful to respected Rev. Dr. Hem Sagar Rasaily, Dr. J.V. Shah and Dr. Philemon Chhetri Khadka. I would like to thank them from the bottom of my heart because they found this book useful and wrote some words of congratulations and encouraged me.

I would like to express my special thanks to Kamal Adhikari, Rakesh Twanabashu, and Bidur Adhikari for helping me get this book completed in English and for designing and editing. I would also like to thank my other loved ones for their prayers, encouragement, and financial support. Since I have been serving outside of Nepal for more than 35 years, there are definitely errors in the language and grammar. I apologize for this and I'm requesting all my readers to correct it and read it.

– Dr. Bishop Dambar Adhikari

Chapter 1

Introduction

MONGOLS AND UNTOUCHABLES

In India, it is understood that the practice of calling Adivasi and *Mulbasi* Dalits or Untouchables happened only after the arrival of the priest of the Baal deity. Even in Nepal, Benei Manasseh's children or their descendants, who geographically have Mongolian faces with small eyes and flat noses, identify that they had twenty-two and twenty-four kingdoms. They did not worship handicrafts. They used to do *Pitri Puja* or worship their dead parents. At that time, the descendants of Benei Ephraim, who were in India, are now called untouchables.

- Both of these communities lived together. Looking at the history, the Vishvakarma community earned their livelihood by making weapons and tools.

- The tanners community provided various types of assistance, such as belts of various leather shoes, and leather. Most of these communities have the surname Mirza. The surname Mirza comes from a place called Armenia. There was a prince named Mirza. Reading the history of Chamars in India also proves that they were once in the Chamar kingdom and a royal family.

The tailor community is not only in existence in Nepal but this surname is called the profession of cloth or sewing clothes. The origin of this surname is also from Turkey. In Turkish Kurdistan, it is called Darzi. In Israel, it is called Talmud and it started specifically in Israel.

So many materials and sources prove that they are descendants of Benei Ephraim. Now, the tailor community plays instruments on the auspicious occasions. Why and how do the priests who carry the ark and Nepal's five musical instruments (*panche baja*) match well.

The priests who eat the tail are another proof. Even though there are so many proofs in the Bible, it can be self-blame for all of us not to believe it. This means that our future generation will have to be lost in the battlefield and wander aimlessly.

SHAH DYNASTY

It is well known that Christians are being persecuted even in the country with the symbol of snake (dangerous snake in the flag). God made all the living things and non-living things. Among the creatures God created, the snake was cunning and it caused Eve and Adam, God's son and daughter, to break the commandment by persuading and misleading them. This is how sin began in the world. Later, God spoke about Jesus being born through the Virgin Mary to conquer Satan, and Jesus was born to crush the head of Satan the serpent. He was crucified, buried in the tomb and rose from the dead. The tomb was emptied and He went to heaven victorious. From the beginning, the desire of the serpent or Satan is to mislead the sons and daughters of God – to separate them from the presence of God and to destroy and to spoil them. Satan is called the father of lies in the Bible.

Similarly, in the beginning, a man named Joseph was sold into Egypt. The children of Joseph increased in number and they were made slaves. The king of Egypt persecuted them viciously. God chose Moses, and through him, He demonstrated many mighty works in the land of Egypt. God brought his people out of Egypt from the hands of Pharaoh and led them into the Promised Land. This struggle was not easy, but God's powerful hand brought them out.

We will concentrate on the pharaoh of Egypt for a few minutes. A host of serpents and a serpent are seen on the crown and throne of the pharaoh. A cobra can be seen in the front part of the crown and cobras can be seen covering the head from behind the throne. Was it the Egyptians or the king of Egypt who were hostile to God, the Creator? Pharaoh did not let God's people go easily. When studying the crowns and thrones of most of the kings in the world, there is a cobra on the crown of the king of Egypt and cobras are also portrayed as protecting the king of Nepal from behind of the throne.

It was there that Pharaoh asked Moses, "I do not know who God is."

It is understood that the deep meaning of this is that I am God myself. Similarly, the Shah Dynasty king of Nepal in the past was also considered as a symbol of Lord Vishnu, and our history shows that the then king also accepted that. How did the heads of the snakes come to the throne of the Shah Dynasty king of Nepal? Probably not everyone knows about this mysterious history or hidden truth about the migration of Pharaoh's children from Egypt to Iraq, Iran, and other Arab countries. The ancestors of our Shah dynasty are found in Iran and Arabia. There were also Shah Dynasty kings in Iran. Although the descendants of those kings lived in India and had Egyptian blood, they became Hindu and entered Nepal and defeated the Mongolian kingdoms – the descendants of Benei Manasseh – and started Vijayadashami. After attacking the Mongolian tribes and directly defeating the Nepali Adivasi, religious laws were imposed starting with Vijayadashami. We need to understand the unknown power of the snake more than the Shah dynasty. We studied a few glimpses before and will do so later that the descendants of Benei Manasseh were Jews.

A woman named Hagar, who was born in Egypt, was Abraham's servant. Abraham's seed Ishmael and the root of Islam are also confirmed to be from Egypt. Christians are persecuted in the Islamic countries. In the same way, our history tells us that Prithvi Narayan Shah exterminated the Adivasi people and deported some Christians and priests.

THE DRAGON IN THE BOOK OF REVELATION

And war broke out in heaven: Michael and his angels fought with the dragon; and the dragon and his angels fought (Revelation 12:7).

Now the beast which I saw was like a leopard, his feet were like the feet of a bear, and his mouth like the mouth of a lion. The dragon gave him his power, his throne, and great authority (Revelation 13:2).

He laid hold of the dragon, that serpent of old, who is the Devil and Satan, and bound him for a thousand years (Revelation 20:2).

And another sign appeared in heaven; behold, a great, fiery red dragon having seven heads and ten horns, and seven diadems on his heads (Revelation 12:3).

There is a deep meaning behind the seven dragon symbols behind the thrones of our past Shah Dynasty kings. The Bible talks about snakes or dragons in many places. So, we don't need much more explanation. The Shah Dynasty kings could not remain stable in any country. They had been persecuting and pestering Jews and Christians since the beginning.

Switzerland, a small country, is one of the richest and strongest countries in the world. There was a struggle before, but the people of the four communities who live there have agreed to make a covenant with God and make the country blessed and stable. A cross has been placed on the flag of their country. Their constitution is also based on the words of the Bible. It has a profound and significant implication.

For example, there are other such countries in the world. Now, America is seen as a very powerful and rich country. The deep secret of this is that if the Israelites who believed in God had not been in America, the country would not prosper. American Christians have understood this secret. We see that America loves and helps Israel through various means. The reason for this is because of the rich and knowledgeable people who are not seen on the frontline. And the people who advise in the parliament are the same Jews. Those who live in our country dream and plan to make it like the Christian country living in America,

Israel, and Europe and send their children to study and work there and dream of developing the country with the grants sent from the Christian countries, but they hound and persecute Nepali Christians living in Nepal. Until the Christians get full rights, there can be no development in the country.

Until we Christians are placed in the first rank of citizens by the state and that behaviour is not done, democracy is and will continue to be just empty words.

ARYAN

Pundit Madhav Prasad Upadhyay has already told us about the arrival of Aryans in his book, Righteousness Exalts a Nation. Although the swastika symbol is dangerous, we will study its religious misuse by Hitler and his symbol or his flag and its meaning. Hitler was also an enemy of the Jews and he killed them in the millions. The swastika symbol also has a mysterious and ominous meaning.

Hitler's aim was to establish his state victory over the world or the whole of Europe.

This swastika symbol is now used as the logo of the later Aryans as well as in various temples. Especially, some Aryans keep this sign in reverse as opposed to Hitler. However, the deeper meaning of all this is that other communities, excluding Aryans, are to be oppressed by rendering them third class citizens.

It is claimed that ninety per cent of communities in India and Nepal believe in the swastika symbol.

But actually, the inner secret of the swastika is more dangerous than the swastika itself. That is why the people of this community strongly oppose the Mongolian tribal community and the Christians, as Hitler did. However, they explain the mystery of the swastika. It is a symbol of the uprooting of the Christians and the descendants of the aboriginal Benei Manasseh.

People who carry this symbol in the world and understand the importance of this symbol are known as Nazi, the ferocious Aryans. According to Pundit Madhav Prasad Upadhyaya, the Aryans were people who quarrelled with God and they were priests to the Baal deity at the time of Elijah.

Let's see from his book; Now, let us try to introduce our ancestors. According to the history of the world, almost all the famous people of the world (foundation of Vedic philosophy) also come to the fore. To know this Vedic book Rigveda. It is necessary to know our mythological history. Our religious history is almost four thousand years old.

shreyan dravya-mayad yajnaj jnana-yajnah parantapa sarvam karmakhilam partha jnane parisamapyate. -Bhagavad Gita 4:33

The best knowledge is knowledge and knowledge gives divine vision. So, let's get out of the veil of ignorance. Only when the veil that entangles us is lifted can we be freed and enlightened by the heavenly master's supernatural power (Matthew 23:10).

1. Jews are very honest. All the countries around us are moving forward. Among them, China is preparing herself to be number one in the world. The India of the Brahmins is getting weaker and weaker. But with the collusion (or agreement) of Westerners and Brahmins, such true news is not allowed to be broadcast outside the media.

2. Aryan Brahmins who ruled India they also admit that they are from the Middle East like the Jews. From this, it can be understood that there is a difference between Jews and Aryan Brahmins.

3. The Jews in India in various non-governmental offices have been ranked.

In this way, honest and simple people have been misled.

I should not wander away from my subject. The true identity of our ancestors is found in the state of slavery with the Hebrew nations and the Jewish nations. These Hebrew people have been referring to our ancestors as Aryans, which will be explained in the coming chapters.

Arya in the Hebrew dictionary means conflict. Another thing to be understood is according to Hebrew history, the Arya society has always been stubborn and stands against its creator and His religious system. American archaeologist Sir Charles Leonard Woolley inspected a mountain called Telamukair in Iraq in 1923 and showed that the Aryans were slaves of the Hebrew people. During the inspection, they found the city of Abraham mentioned in the Bible. Abraham's four-storey houses and worship houses built for daily use were also found in this small but orderly city. Small houses where the servants lived as well as Abraham's office to keep the accounts of everything were also found. The calculation of the amount of money that would come to Abraham's family for serving God annually and being the head of the group was clearly mentioned therein.

The account of the gold, silver and money to be given to the slave-servants and the names of the slave-servants who received their wages were filed in the parchment leather writing paper. In that file, there was also the name of the servants and the family name. Behind each name was clearly written Arya-Arya-Arya. The house was so intact that fire could was often be rekindled in the kitchen of Abraham's nearly four-thousand-year-old house by these archaeologists.

Glyn Edmund Daniel writes in Encyclopaedia Britannica: The clay tablets were found in the residential quarter of the city, of which a considerable area was excavated. The houses of private citizens in the Larsa period and under Hammurabi of Babylon (c. 18th century BCE, in which period Abraham is supposed to have lived at Ur) were comfortable and well-built two-story houses with ample accommodation for the family, for servants, and for guests, of a type that ensured privacy and was suited to the climate. In some houses was a kind of chapel in which the family god was worshipped and under the pavement of which members of the family were buried. Many large state temples were excavated, as were some small wayside shrines dedicated by private persons to minor deities, the latter throwing a new light upon Babylonian religious practices; but the domestic chapels, with their provision for the worship of the nameless family gods, are yet more interesting and have a possible relation to the religion of the Hebrew patriarchs. (Daniel, Glyn Edmund. "archaeology". Encyclopaedia Britannica)

It has been proven that the priests of Baal deity who survived hiding in different corners of the land escaped from Israel and came to India through Palestine, Iran, Iraq, and Afghanistan and then entered Nepal. In the Hebrew dictionary, Arya means a person who fights with God. Down through centuries, the differences, disharmony, and disunity between the four communities have led to a great dispersal and dissension among the people.

In order to break down these walls and to come to an agreement and an understanding, various organizations have been set up and agreements are being signed on various documents. Even after so many attempts and struggles, this (casteist) communal conflict continues to lead to more and more complications. One day, this struggle may likely turn our (four castes) four communities into a battlefield, and our heavenly garden of a nation may burn into ashes. The main reason is the true history of our past being turned into a fairy tale and the resultant division of the community. According to the fairy tale, Brahma made five types of people and there is an attempt to smear this creation by bringing differences in the name of religion. As I have stated above, the Mongolian community and touchable community were the first inhabitants, and history has also proved it. I have already said that the Mongolians are the descendants of the Benei Manasseh and are the first people. History has also proved it.

I have already presented evidence that the Mongolians are descendants of Benei Manasseh. Both of these communities lived together until the time of Prithvi Narayan Shah, and during war time, these tailors, craftsmen, and leather-worker (tanner) communities had a great role in making army uniforms, tools, weapons, and shoes. In India and Nepal, especially the children of Benei Ephraim and Benei Israel are called the lost tribe. They are given the name Harijan. In Sanskrit, Hari means the creator and Jana means offspring or descendants.

In India, these Harijans are forbidden from entering temples and touching cooked food. Because Mahatma Gandhi had read the Bible, he often said that these Harijan are the sons and daughters of God. He repeatedly spoke in favour of them, saying that the injustice should be stopped. Later, they were named Dalit. In Nepal, the word untouchable has been used in the society since the beginning and there are mostly these three communities and various small communities within them. Besides, they are forbidden from entering temples and they are also forbidden from entering the house of the so-called upper caste and touching their cooked food. Why?

In various places in the Bible, the Israelites are forbidden to touch unclean things, corpses, and the dead body. These communities who are known as untouchables do not bow down to idols and they should not be touched by idol worshippers. A cloth maker is called a tailor. Actually, its correct pronunciation (*Siojikar*) is also known as darjee in needlework or master ji. If we become untouchables because of sewing clothes, then our ancestor Adam first made clothes from leaves and covered the nakedness of both Adam and Eve. Because Adam was the first father, we are all children of Adam.

If we say that those who work with leather should be called untouchables then we need to reckon with the fact that God himself made leather clothes. The LORD God made tunics of skins for Adam and his wife and clothed them (Genesis 3:21).

Paul and Peter were tanners. Tanners wrote the Words of the Bible. To write the Bible, they used: Skin of sheep, goats, and deer

- Skin of a calf of a belin cow

Therefore, if these leather workers are untouchable, God himself is also untouchable.

CRAFTSMEN IN THE BIBLE

Then, the Lord spoke to Moses, saying, "See, I have called by name Bezalel the son of Uri, the son of Hur, of the tribe of Judah." (Exodus 31:1-2).

And Moses said to the children of Israel, "See, the Lord has called by name Bezalel the son of Uri, the son of Hur, of the tribe of Judah." (Exodus 35:30).

Then, Moses called Bezalel, the son of Uri, the grandson of Judah's tribe of Hur, the tailor, the tanner, the craftsman. Here below it is mentioned as the blacksmith.

"Behold, I have created the blacksmith who blows the coals in the fire, who brings forth an instrument for his work. And I have created the spoiler to destroy. No weapon formed against you shall prosper, and every tongue which rises against you in judgment you shall condemn. This is the heritage of the servants of the Lord, and their righteousness is from Me," says the Lord. (Isaiah 54:16-17)

Behold, I have created the blacksmith who blows the coals in the fire, who brings forth an instrument for his work. And I have created the spoiler to destroy. In the old days, the Bible was burned several times, but if the sculptors had not written the Bible on metal and buried it in the ground, we would not have the word of God in our hands today. In India, they are being called Vishwakarma or to worship Vishwakarma indicates that these communities have the gift of engineering and are skilled; they are like the Lord because the karma of the world is in their hands. But in Nepal, they are called untouchables.

The surnames of the entire untouchable community that we have studied above and the surnames of the Aryas are not the same but are found to be very similar.

1. The first arrivals were Mongol aborigines

2. Second arrivals were the so-called Untouchable community

3. Shah Dynasty

4. Aryas

Most of the surnames of the untouchable community have appeared in many other communities and have come into circulation. This proves that this community was already here in Nepal before the arrival of other communities, and from the surname of this community, it can be deduced that some surnames have been adopted by other communities.

Chapter 2

A Mongolian History

AAKHAYAN (NARRATIVE)

1. Geographically, Nepal is located between Tibet/China and India. These two neighbours of Nepal represent two communities.

   Mongols from Tibet and intellectual Aryans from India- it can be generally assumed that Nepalis are a hybrid of these two powers.

   This is the truth. Now the question is, Who came first in Nepal between the Mongols and Aryans?

2. In Aakhayan Page No. 7-8

   According to the estimation of the time, both *Haplo* groups G2a2 M9a1a2a seem to be about 6,000 years old. According to the study, the age of North Eastern Europeans is about 8 years.

   It seems that it is known in Tibet. These studies seem to be consistent with the estimated time and dating frame. From this, we can agree that the East Europeans came to Nepal about 6000 years ago across the Himalayas. Both archaeology and linguistics agree on this issue.

   Before the Aryans came here, the Tibetan Mongols had entered Nepal across the Himalayas. "These three were the sons of Noah, and from these the whole earth was populated" (Genesis 9:19). "And the border of the Canaanites was from Sidon as you go toward Gerar, as far as Gaza; then as you go toward Sodom, Gomorrah, Admah, and Zeboiim, as far as Lasha" (Genesis 10: 19).

Source: (Bible Journey, Page No.162-163, Author Balkumari). Now this is the genealogy of the sons of Noah: Shem, Ham, and Japheth. And sons were born to them after the flood.

THE SONS OF JAPHETH

The sons of Japheth were Gomer, Magog, Madai, Javan, Tubal, Meshech, and Tiras. The sons of Gomer were Ashkenaz, Riphath, and Togarmah. The sons of Javan were Elishah, Tarshish, Kittim, and Dodanim. From these, the coastland peoples of the Gentiles were separated into their lands, everyone according to his language, according to their families, into their nations. The sons of Ham were Cush, Mizraim, Put, and Canaan. The sons of Cush were Seba, Havilah, Sabtah, Raamah, and Sabtechah; and the sons of Raamah were Sheba and Dedan Cush begot Nimrod; he began to be a mighty one on the earth. He was a mighty hunter before the Lord; therefore, it is said, "Like Nimrod, the mighty hunter before the Lord." And the beginning of his kingdom was Babel, Erech, Accad, and Calneh, in the land of Shinar. From that land, he went to Assyria and built Nineveh, Rehoboth Ir, Calah, and Resen between Nineveh and Calah (that is the principal city). Mizraim begot Ludim, Anamim, Lehabim, Naphtuhim, Pathrusim, and Casluhim (from whom came the Philistines and Caphtorim). Canaan begot Sidon his firstborn, and Heth; the Jebusite, the Amorite, and the Girgashite; the Hivite, the Arkite, and the Sinite; the Arvadite, the Zemarite, and the Hamathite. Afterward the families of the Canaanites were dispersed. And the border of the Canaanites was from Sidon as you go toward Gerar, as far as Gaza; then as you go toward Sodom, Gomorrah, Admah, and Zeboiim, as far as Lasha. These were the sons of Ham, according to their families, according to their languages, in their lands and in their nations. And children were born also to Shem, the father of all the children of Eber, the brother of Japheth the elder. The sons of Shem were Elam, Asshur, Arphaxad, Lud, and Aram. The sons of Aram were Uz, Hul, Gether, and Mash. Arphaxad begot Salah, and Salah begot Eber. To Eber were born two sons: the name of one was Peleg, for in his days the earth was divided, and his brother's name was Joktan. Joktan begot Almodad, Sheleph, Hazarmaveth, Jerah, Hadoram, Uzal, Diklah, Obal, Abimael, Sheba, Ophir, Havilah, and Jobab. All these were the sons of Joktan. And their dwelling place was from Mesha as you go toward Sephar, the mountain of the east. These were the sons of Shem, according to their families, according to their languages, in their lands, according to their nations (Genesis 10:1-32).

Noah had three sons.

Japheth, Ham and Shem.

DESCENDANTS OF SHEM

Shem means wheat. The descendants of Shem went to the east and settled in Asia and from them arose five communities.

1. Elam

2. Assyria

3. Arpachashad

4. Lud

5. Aram

Shem Eber (Hebrew) was the progenitor of all the children of the Hebrews. Especially, he was the progenitor of the Israelites through Arpachashad. The Jews arose through him. Abraham was the patriarch of the Jews and in his time, they migrated from eastern Ur to Palestine, a country originally called Canaan but later called Israel after the second name of Jacob, Abraham's grandson).

21 And children were born also to Shem, the father of all the children of Eber, the brother of Japheth the elder. 22 The sons of Shem were Elam, Asshur, Arphaxad, Lud, and Aram. 23The sons of Aram were Uz, Hul, Gether, and Mash. 24 Arphaxad begot Salah, and Salah begot Eber. 25 To Eber were born two sons: the name of one was Peleg, for in his days the earth was divided; and his brother's name was Joktan. 26 Joktan begot Almodad, Sheleph, Hazarmaveth, Jerah, 27Hadoram,

Uzal, Diklah, 28 Obal, Abimael, Sheba, 29 Ophir, Havilah, and Jobab. All these were the sons of Joktan. 30 And their dwelling place was from Mesha as you go toward Sephar, the mountain of the east. 31These were the sons of Shem, according to their families, according to their languages, in their lands, according to their nations (Genesis 10:21-31).

Sons of Shem. These verses describe the descendants of Shem, who went to settle in Arabia and the Middle Eastern valleys.

Jews, Assyrians, Syrians and Elamites belong to them. Perhaps, light brownish (*Shyamvan Gahugoro*) people who are popular in Nepal, may have been recognized on the basis of this.

DESCENDANTS OF HAM

Ham means 'black.' They settled mostly in the south, in North-Africa and Palestine, and from them arose four communities.

1.   Cush

2.   Mizraim

3.   Put

4.   Canaan

They were famous for being able to consume heat in summer season. Ham insulted his father by seeing his nakedness and lost his authority and blessing and the cursed dynasty began.

Even in Nepal, many people tend to harm the honour, dignity, and prestige of others by insulting and pulling the legs of others. Perhaps, we have societies that contain the blood and semen of the cursed people of Africa?

DESCENDANTS OF JAPHETH

The meaning of Japheth is "white" or "white face." Most of them went west and settled in Europe, but some families also went to live in Asia. From these arose (seven) communities:

1. Gomer

2. Magog

3. Madai

4. Javan

5. Tubal

6. Meshech

7. Tiras

They became the Aryan community and they were famous for their intellectual knowledge. (Bible Journey, p. 163)

The children of Madai listed in number 12 above are found in abundance in the Bible. (In Esther 1:3 they are pronounced Media.)

"Parthians and Medes and Elamites, those dwelling in Mesopotamia, Judea and Cappadocia, Pontus and Asia" (Acts 2:10). Here the Holy Spirit is also poured out on Medes.

2 "The sons of Japheth were Gomer, Magog, Madai, Javan, Tubal, Meshech, and Tiras. 3 The sons of Gomer were Ashkenaz, Riphath, and Togarmah. 4 The sons of Javan were Elishah, Tarshish, Kittim, and Dodanim. 5 From these the coastland peoples of the Gentiles were separated into their lands, everyone according to his language, according to their families, into their nations" (Genesis 10:2-5).

These verses describe the descendants of Japheth. They went to the north to settle on the shores of the Black Sea and the Caspian Sea. They later became the ancestors of the Medes, Greeks as well as the Indo-European white people of Europe and Asia.

As the history of the Medes unfolds, the book of Jonah in the Bible and the city of Nineveh has to be mentioned. To this city which God loves and saves, He sent the prophet Jonah to allow them to repent.

The people of Nineveh are similar to the Assyrians and various communities, as well as Medes and Nepalese, especially their customs, instruments, and language are similar to the *"sagune"* or priestly musician community of Nepal.

All these researches were carried out by myself, various personalities, who have now lost their country Kurdistan and have been living in different parts of the world. Among them, I have researched the language of a Kurdistan animal doctor Farhan who is living in Syria:

Writing	Speaking	Nepali	English	
Kurdis	Kurdis	Kurdis	Language	
Mall	Mahal	Ghar	Building	1
Seher	Ser	Sher	Lion	2
Massi	Machhi	Machha	Fish	3
Sev	Sew	Syau	Apple	4

Azman	Ajman	Asman	Sky	5
Harth, Hard	Artha	Jamin	Earth	6
Malek	Malik	Raja	King	7
Mehwan	Mehawan	Pahuna	Guest	8
Daod	Daod	Janti	Wedding Procession	9
Deu	Deu	Dahi	Curd	10
Nazek	Najik	Najik	Near	11
Dur	Dur	Tadha	Far	12
Khuse	Khusi	Khusi Hunu	Happy	13
Hajar	Hajar	Hajar	Thousand	14
Bis	Bis	Bis	Twenty	15
Suve	Subhe	Bihana	Morning	16
Dil	Dil	Hridaya	Heart	17
Zakmak	Chakmak	Chakmak	Shining	18
Khude	Khude	Parmeshor	God	19
BArkat	Barkat	Ashish	Blessing	20
Khune	Khune	Khun	Blood	21

Mahhabat	Mahabbat	Pyar	Love	22
Salam	Salam	Salam	Shalom	23
Zernai	Sahanahi	Sahanahi	Instrument	24
Cas	Jas	Jhymta	Cymbal	25
Panir	Panir	Chij	Cheese	26
Khatar	Khatar	Khatara	Danger	27
Majak	Majak	Maja Garnu	Teasing	28
Tarjuma	Tarjuma	Anuwad	Translation	29
Kitab	Kitab	Pustak	Book	30
Gost	Gost	Masu	Meat	31
Chae	Chaya	Chiya	Tea	32
Sekhar	Shekhar	Sakhhar	Sugar	33
Hawa	Hawa	Batas	Wind	34
Nan	Nan	Roti	Bread	35
Khai	Khyal	Khalkhalko	Various	36

Seri	Seri	Shir	Head	37
Kurban	Kurban	Bhog Dinu	Sacrifice	38
Terzi	Darji	Vastra Banaune	Tailor	39
Zarma	Charma	Chala	Skin	40
Attar	Attar	Basna	Scent	41

The estimated dispersion of Nineveh city is similar in Nepali language and most of them are Jews in Israel and about 50 million in Turkey, about 11 million in Iran, about 8 million in Iraq, about 3 million in Syria and about 2 million in Europe. Sanahi, a kind of instrument, is also played in the auspicious ceremony of marriage and those who dance and play the instrument take money from the bride and groom as well as the whole people, but the one who makes the instrument play is not forced.

In Nepal, they go and after reaching the bride's house. They don't know that they spend the night with theatre and revelry all night and when they come with the bride to the groom's house playing five instruments, those who are invited to the whole party give money.

Now, we will again show some evidence and basis about how this system came to be in Nepal.

According to Esther chapter 1 of the Bible and Aakhayan secular resource, the above biblical foundations seem to match the assumptions of secular research. Now, we will enter another base again.

"Now it came to pass in the days of Ahasuerus (this was the Ahasuerus who reigned over one hundred and twenty-seven provinces, from India to Ethiopia)" (Esther 1:1).

At that time, ruling over one hundred and twenty-seven province-countries was not an ordinary thing. Although it looks like countries in Asia, Cush means a place from Bible Dictionary 175, possibly an area in Asia. "The name of the second river is Gihon; it is the one which goes around the whole land of Cush" (Genesis 2:13). The area south of Eden and southern Egypt (Nubia or North Sudan): Classical writers call it Ethiopia, and some Bible translations use this term. But this is not modern Ethiopia. In the old covenant, this was closely associated with Egypt.

"And the king heard concerning Tirhakah king of Ethiopia, 'He has come out to make war with you.' So, when he heard it, he sent messengers to Hezekiah" (Isaiah 37:9). Both of these places had the same king named Tirhakah. The topaz used to come from this place. "The topaz of Ethiopia cannot equal it, nor can it be valued in pure gold." (Job 28:19). The people of this place were black in colour.

"Can the Ethiopian change his skin or the leopard its spots? Then may you also do good who are accustomed to do evil." (Jeremiah 13:23). Similarly, a person with great authority under Candace the queen also came from this place. Here, I am trying to show all the basic proofs so that the readers might not have doubts and curiosity.

Since Persia ruled over the whole of Asia and Africa at that time, some people used to come here and there with different types of trade. At the same time, some Mongolian Jews also immigrated to different Asia and settled in a mixed family home, so shouldn't the Jews be only white skinned? It is natural to ask this question. That is why the Jews scattered all over the world.

At that time, doing business was not as easy as it is now. Crossing one sea from another sea by ship, horse, camel, and taking goods from one country to another could be difficult and time-consuming. In the same way, the word India has been seen long before through Iran, Iraq, Israel, and Afghanistan. Therefore, it is difficult to estimate the exact date when Mongolians and Jews entered Nepal, but they did enter.

Mongolian friends were ancestor worshipers and nature worshipers. Our God loves all the people of the whole world. Come, surrender your life to Jesus, receive eternal life and become children of the living God.

Also, Harijan, please come in the presence of God. Give thanks to my dear Brahmin Pundits. Stop committing the deadly sin of idolatry and trust Jesus as your Saviour. Don't compromise the society by building a god-house and placing a tika (sectarian mark) on the forehead that will make the society happy. God has protected you from generation to generation. Forcibly entering someone else's temple is a violation of their human rights. Trying to enter someone's house without someone else's permission is a violation of their human rights. Today, stop making all these accusations that your human rights have been violated!

I have a suggestion for the senior pastors and Bible teachers of my Christian church that when you set an example, stop the habit of calling the holy people from the Harijan community as Samaritans in the church. Because comparing Dalits with Samaritans is unbiblical. The Samaritans became impure or untouchable because they worshiped idols. Jews are not idolaters; they worship the true God. "29 However every nation continued to make gods of its own, and put them in the shrines on the high places which the Samaritans had made, every nation in the cities where they dwelt. 30 The men of Babylon made Succoth Benoth, the men of Cuth made Nergal, the men of Hamath made Ashima, 31 and the Avites made Nibhaz and Tartak; and the Sepharvites burned their children in fire to Adrammelech and Anammelech, the gods of Sepharvaim. 32 So they feared the Lord, and from every class they appointed for themselves priests of the high places, who sacrificed for them in the shrines of the high places" (2 Kings 17:29-32).

INSTEAD OF THE ISRAELITES THEY WERE SETTLED IN THE CITIES OF SAMARIA

The king of Assyria brought other foreign prisoners to settle in the cities of Samaria (that is, the entire northern kingdom) in order to destroy the little nationality left in them. There was no intermarriage between the Israelites taken to Assyria and the Assyrians, but the foreigners who were brought to Israel intermarried with the Israelites there, and their mixed children born to foreigners were called Samaritans.

We find that these people made various deities who ate food and sacrificed their sons and daughters. Because of doing these kinds of disgusting things, they became Samaritan. That is why it is a wrong teaching to always call the Dalits Samaritans in our church and to frequently address those who have come to faith from the Dalit community as Samaritans.

- Don't forget the background that once you were alcohol drinking and a god worshiping people. Then, you became Pastors.

- Don't forget that Pastors who came from the Brahmin Pundits (priests) community are also forgiven by God. Once you were idol worshippers. Idol worship, ancestor worship is an abominable and despicable sin. Now, all the children of God and the Harijans are the children of the same father. Looking at the background, these are all descendants of Benei Manasseh. These Jews are being sent to their country of Israel. Not all Jews have big eyes and pointed noses, because of geographical climate, there are all kinds of Jews in the world, just like the people with many faces in Nepal.

Even though they have been living outside Israel for centuries, they do not worship idols just like the Dalit untouchables in Nepal who don't worship idols. Just as Dalits in Nepal do not marry with other communities, neither do they. Just as Dalits are not allowed to worship idols, they are also not allowed to worship idols. Just as the Star of David is made of rice flour during various festivals of the Dalits of Nepal, they also have their own Jewish rituals. After David ruled the kingdom, the royal symbol, the hexagon, the Israeli flag, and the Mongolian flag entered various logos in Nepal during the untouchable time. The swastika symbol is the symbol of the Aryan race, with which Hitler of Germany killed the Jews. These symbols were later brought into Nepal by the Aryan caste. With various logos, Mongolians from outside Nepal reached the moon and ate momo (dumpling), Japanese Mongolians surprised the world by excelling in electrical and technical fields as well as manufacturing cars, trains, education and geographical development. The Chinese are drawing the world towards themselves by developing geography, materials, tools, weapons, plants. There are other countries that have not been influenced by the Aryans. My beloved Mongolians of our country remained silent when others occupied the land they had been living in.

Now, you insult our Brahmins and say that they did not let us read. You insult them by saying that we honest and simple people were called Gurung. If you feel inferior in your surname, edit it without writing Gurung's caste and there are many other surnames. The law does not allow changing the surname, but it can be done by following the process to amend it. Now all Mongolians, my dear ones, get education like the Japanese and Chinese. Stop insulting, reprimanding and threatening my Arya Brahmins.

AAKHYAN (NARRATIVE)

Geographically, Nepal is located between Tibet (China) and India. These two neighbours of Nepal represent the two species (Ethnicity). Mongols came from Tibet and Aryans from India. From this, it can be generally intellectually assumed that the Nepalese are the hybrid of these two species. This is the truth. Now, the question arises as to who among the Mongols and the Aryans came to Nepal first.

According to the estimation of the time, both *haplo* groups G2a2/Mga1a2a seem to be about 6,000 years old. According to the study, the age of North Eastern Europeans is about 8200 years 8.2 kya (Zhao et al). It seems that it is known in Tibet in about 2009. These studies seem to be consistent with the estimated time and dating frame. From this, we can agree that the East Europeans came to Nepal about 6,000 years ago across the Himalayas. Both archeology and linguistics have agreed on this matter. Before Aryans came to Nepal, Tibetan Mongols had entered Nepal across the Himalayas.

There were Jews in Persia at that time, from Esther 1 chapter, which tells about Noah's son from the Bible journey. At that time, there were 127 countries in Asia.

The city of Nineveh was big before and the ancestors of the people who kept the map are Madis. They are found in various places in the Bible.

How did these Jews enter China and other Asian countries from Iran? The practice of Sanai, Darzi, who gives information, comes from Nineveh and Turkey.

GENETIC ANCESTRY OF NEPALESE

Geographically, Nepal is located between China (Tibet) and India. In Nepal, these two neighbours represent two species (ethnicity).

TIBET MONGOLS AND ARYANS FROM INDIA

From this, it can be generally intellectually assumed that Nepalese are the hybrid of these species, which is the truth. Now the question arises who came first among Mongols and Aryans in Nepal?

According to the estimation of the time, both haplo groups G292/mga1a2a seem to be about 6,000 years old. According to the study, the age of North Eastern Europeans is about 8200 years 8.2 kya (Zhao et al, 2009). These studies seem to be consistent with the estimated time and dating frame. From this we can agree that the East Eurasians came to Nepal about 6000 years ago through the Himalayas. Both archaeology and linguistics have agreed on this matter. Before Aryans came to Nepal, Tibetan Mongols had entered Nepal from the Himalayas.

THE BIBLE JOURNEY IS TOLD FROM NOAH'S SON Now it came to pass in the days of Ahasuerus (this was the Ahasuerus who reigned over one hundred and twenty-seven provinces, from India to Ethiopia), 2 in those days when King Ahasuerus sat on the throne of his kingdom, which was in Shushan the citadel, 3 that in the third year of his reign he made a feast for all his officials and servants—the powers of Persia and Media, the nobles, and the princes of the provinces being before him — 4 when he showed the riches of his glorious kingdom and the splendor of his excellent majesty for many days, one hundred and eighty days in all.

5 And when these days were completed, the king made a feast lasting seven days for all the people who were present in Shushan the citadel, from great to small, in the court of the garden of the king's palace. 6 There were white and blue linen curtains fastened with cords of fine linen and purple on silver rods and marble pillars; and the couches were of gold and silver on a mosaic pavement of alabaster, turquoise, and white and black marble. 7 And they served drinks in golden vessels, each vessel being different from the other, with royal wine in abundance, according to the generosity of the king. 8 In accordance with the law, the drinking

was not compulsory; for so the king had ordered all the officers of his household, that they should do according to each man's pleasure.

9 Queen Vashti also made a feast for the women in the royal palace which belonged to King Ahasuerus.

10 On the seventh day, when the heart of the king was merry with wine, he commanded Mehuman, Biztha, Harbona, Bigtha, Abagtha, Zethar, and Carcas, seven eunuchs who served in the presence of King Ahasuerus, 11 to bring Queen Vashti before the king, wearing her royal crown, in order to show her beauty to the people and the officials, for she was beautiful to behold. 12 But Queen Vashti refused to come at the king's command brought by his eunuchs; therefore the king was furious, and his anger burned within him.

13 Then the king said to the wise men who understood the times (for this was the king's manner toward all who knew law and justice, 14 those closest to him being Carshena, Shethar, Admatha, Tarshish, Meres, Marsena, and Memucan, the seven princes of Persia and Media, who had access to the king's presence, and who ranked highest in the kingdom): 15 "What shall we do to Queen Vashti, according to law, because she did not obey the command of King Ahasuerus brought to her by the eunuchs?"

16 And Memucan answered before the king and the princes: "Queen Vashti has not only wronged the king, but also all the princes, and all the people who are in all the provinces of King Ahasuerus. 17 For the queen's behaviour will become known to all women, so that they will despise their husbands in their eyes, when they report, 'King Ahasuerus commanded Queen Vashti to be brought in before him, but she did not come.' 18 This very day the noble ladies of Persia and Media will say to all the king's officials that they have heard of the behavior of the queen. Thus, there will be excessive contempt and wrath. 19 If it pleases the king, let a royal decree go out from him, and let it be recorded in the laws of the Persians and the Medes, so that it will not be altered, that Vashti shall come no more before King Ahasuerus; and let the king give

her royal position to another who is better than she. 20 When the king's decree which he will make is proclaimed throughout all his empire (for it is great), all wives will honour their husbands, both great and small."

21 And the reply pleased the king and the princes, and the king did according to the word of Memucan. 22 Then he sent letters to all the king's provinces, to each province in its own script, and to every people in their own language, that each man should be master in his own house, and speak in the language of his own people. (Esther 1:1-22) At that time, there were Jews in Persia and at that time there were 127 countries in Asia. It was a vast Asian country. Once the city of Nineveh was large. The ancestors of the people here are Medes. Medes are found in various places in the Bible. The people of Nineveh also play Sanai (an instrument) and Panchebaja (five instruments) at weddings and other auspicious events, and the community that dances and sings at weddings has a tradition of making people happy and collecting money with their mouths. Earlier, in different parts of Nepal, the bridegroom and the bride used to play musical instruments in the house of the bridegroom and the people and the audience were happy with the musical thrill and asked for money. Here in Turkish Kurdistan, people who sew clothes are called tailors. We find a lot of similarities in Hindi, Urdu and Nepali language of people of Turkey and Kurdistan.

BENE EPHRAIM (IN HEBREW A SON OF EPHRAIM)

They are also known as Telugu Jews. These Jews speak Telugu language and declare that they too are the lost children of Ephraim. They live outside the village of Kottaredding Palem, Guntur of Andhra Pradesh, on the banks of the Krishna River Delta. They declare that Israel came from Asia: Persia, Afghanistan, Tibet, and China 1,600 years ago and South India 1,000 years ago and they started writing history like the Bene Manasseh. Mizoram and Manipur got a letter from the Chief Rabbi of Israel. After that, they completed the legal process and prepared for Israeli citizenship. During the medieval period, these Jews used to do very hard work. For example, they used to do farming and menial jobs.

But later, after they heard the gospel of Christ Jesus through the British missionaries, they became baptized Christians and accepted Christ Jesus.

This proves that there are as many poor untouchables in Nepal as possible. These are their descendants. They may have already come to Nepal. But later, their leader, Samuel Yacovi, went to Jerusalem and in 1980, he convinced that they were of Jewish descent.

Because for a long time, some religious practices of the Jews as well as cultures were not seen in the practice and no evidence was revealed in the society. There was no evidence.

These Jews could not show evidence of their lineage. They did not speak the Jewish language or any words. But they spoke only Telugu language. (See Jews languages).

In 1980, about fifty families started studying Jewish language in the nearby districts of Lottareddipalem/Ongole and then, they built their own synagogues. Now, the whole world has proven the Jews to be poor and enslaved wage labourers doing low-level jobs. Most of the time, they practice their Judaism in Hebrew. But the Chief Priest of Israel, Chief Rabbi did not agree to certify them as Jews. Perhaps, in my opinion, the DNA blood test did not give proof. Even in Nepal, now untouchable communities can be descendants of Bene Ephraim. Because these are the communities that have not worshiped idols for hundreds of years. Many speculate that they may have come to India from Israel through different countries to save the lives of the children of Bene Ephraim. In my opinion, their children may have also entered Nepal.

The Jews of India are not all the same; they are different. Due to being in different groups, there are different customs and lifestyles. There are also different customs and different clothes among them. They provide evidence that there are three types of Jews in India.

2000 YEARS AGO, THEY CAME AND SETTLED IN INDIA

Cochin Jews settled in Kerala, South India and they are dark-skinned Jews. Now, it is one of the most rich and intelligent as well as developed provinces of India. Their surnames are often found to be Thomas, Elijah, Joseph, and Zacharias – the same biblical names – and they are mostly Christians. Another type of Iraqi Jews claim themselves as Baghdadi Jews and that in the eighteenth century, they migrated from Iraq to India, particularly Bombay and Calcutta, and settled there. They used to be yellow in colour and now, their skin changed due to the weather of India and they are also often found to be skilled in business.

THIRD TYPE OF THE JEWS

Achkenazi Jews went to Manipur, India and settled there. They claim that they are the descendants of one of the lost tribes and they are the children of Bene Manasseh and they also have their own kind of synagogues.

The Bene Manasseh (a son of Israel) claim to be the sons of Israel. In the second century BC, they came from Galilee and settled in Bombay, Calcutta, Old Delhi, and Ahmedabad. Their language became Marathi. Bene Israel does not look like Jews. They are Marathas and they started marrying Indians and Jews and the children born from them look like our Nepali Rai, Limbu, Gurung, Magar, Sherpa, and Tamang, and they also have a more focused practice in Jewish culture. The aboriginal people of Nepal are found to be of Mongolian appearance. Many of them have also gone to Israel. They can be said to be the first people who entered Nepal. They started to produce oil as well as other tools by tending sheep and cultivating crops. Their sure history is found in Navgaon. The fact that they are Jews is evidenced by their preference for the Sabbath day on Saturday. From Navgaon, they migrated and settled in many other areas.

Attested names like Rohekar, Penkar, Palkar, Asthamkar Roha, Pen, and Pali Astham came into contact with the Bene Israelite Cochin Jews in the 17th century and later, migrated to Bombay with Bene Israel in Modern Jews. And together with these, Bene Israel became a strong, popular opinion in a very powerful growing population. Their number grew to 30,000 by 1948. Today, there are 5,000 in India. More and more have returned to Israel. Some (in Australia) are in intelligence agencies in England and many government offices and also in the Indian Army. But in the years 1950 and 1960, a large number of Jews returned to Israel and the remaining Jews are in the famous Modern Community in Mumbai.

Most Indians with Christian surnames say that they were Dalits and now they have converted to Christianity. But this is not true. They were a group of Jews who did not worship idols, but the idol worshipers made accusations like this. However, according to my experience and research, they are now the untouchables of Nepal or the ancestors of the untouchables of Nepal. These three types of Indian Jews are even better.

Flag of the Jews

The Star of David, also called the Seal of Solomon, is an equidistant hexagon. It seems to have gained almost universal significance across cultures and civilizations. Many educational institutions and universities use the hexagon in their logo. Similarly, army and sports institutions also use it.

Stars and especially the North Star, used to be a guidance or reference point for navigators before the compass was invented.

The star is a symbol of light and guidance, strength and victory. It signifies the antidote to darkness and chaos, a guide amidst disorientation and purposelessness. The wide-spread significance attests to the enduring significance of the hexagonal star.

HEXAGON AND SWASTIKA SYMBOL

These two symbols are more popular in Nepal and especially in Hindu society, but it is important to know about their source and meaning in other countries.

- After David ruled the kingdom, he used the royal symbol, the hexagon, to remember the king.

  Therefore, nowadays, this symbol is the flag of the country of Israel and the symbol of Judaism, just as the symbol of Christianity is the cross.

- But in the Second World War, the evil leader of Germany, Hitler, forced all the Jews to put on the hexagon sign and by this they were humiliated. Most of the people were killed.

- The same sign seems to be used as an auspicious sign by Hindus today. But Nepali Christians use this sign only as a logo of an organization.

- This swastika symbol is the symbol of the Aryan race.

- But during the Second World War, the evil leader of Germany, Hitler, adopted this sign to show his German race as the pure Aryan race. German soldiers wearing swastikas persecuted Jews wearing hexagons and killed many Jews.

- The same sign seems to be used as an auspicious sign by Hindus today. Maybe, some Nepali Christians use this sign without knowing it.

Although these two signs are considered as lucky and auspicious signs in Nepal, as mentioned above, these two signs are seen very differently in European countries. Although the hexagon symbol indicates the Jews, it is not considered to be an auspicious symbol, but the swastika symbol is considered a very evil and disgusting symbol and no Christian should use it as a religious symbol.

Chapter 3

The History of Untouchablity

TAILORING

The first use of the Hebrew word 'tailor' is found in the Messianic or Midrashim literature. There is frequent mention of people who sew clothes (tailors) in Talmud as well. At one time, Jews used to sew clothes in small numbers in Muslim countries. Almost every Jewish community needed their own tailors. And they were required to observe the religious ordinance such as *shaatnez*. The church also encouraged this and seemed they were willing to wear the special Jewish clothing.

The term 'tailoring' also came to be understood as giving money as a pawn for good repair. In Muslim countries, there was no such thing as lending and borrowing money. Small and mid-level tailoring was of great importance in Jewish society.

By 1948, everyone used to weave and sew clothes in the Jewish village of Yemen. In medieval Europe, guilds used to cause a lot of trouble to the Jewish tailors. They hindered the making of special and different clothes for the Jews.

In Italy and especially in Rome, second-hand goods and old clothes were repaired to be sold. The Jewish tailors were seen in the repair of clothes from the 15th century. In the 16th century, as much as a quarter or a half Jews seem to be involved in the cloth trade business in various areas. Bernardino Ramazzini (1633-1714) was the first authority to study occupational disease. He said that many Jews had weak eyes, legs and lungs. The main reason for all this is that the house has little light and narrow windows, so the air is low and old clothes are made in such a place. Doing so has affected their health. (Cited in Riva, MA, et al.)

It is less known that the first observations on the effects of metals on the nervous system can be found in the "De Morbis Artificum Diatriba" by the Italian physician, Bernardino Ramazzini (1633–1714). In chapter VII ("Diseases of glass-workers and mirror-makers") of his masterpiece, Ramazzini described the effects of mercury on motor function and mood, stating: "Those who make mirrors, using mercury, become palsied [...]. These workers with grim expression (torvis oculis) contemplate the reflection of their suffering in the very mirrors they have made with their own hands and curse the profession they have had to follow."

Furthermore, in chapter IX, he explained that painters were afflicted by palsy of the limbs, caused by colours of mineral origin containing pigments of mercury, lead and copper. These statements indicate a first medical and scientific acknowledgment that exposure to toxic agents can cause both physical and behavioural alterations; therefore, Ramazzini can be considered as a pioneer of neurotoxicology.

In Central Europe, as elsewhere, Jewish tailoring was bound by the laws of the shaatnez. It was related to repairing and selling old clothes.

There was a great difference of opinion between the Christians and the Jewish guilds in Prague because of the accusations of illegally selling new clothes to the Jewish tailors. Due to this dispute, the Prague community was expelled in the year 1745. The expelled Jews went from village to village and started producing cloth so that no one came to buy new cloth in Prague. Due to this situation, the Christian tailors also got affected.

In 1418, among the Jewish families, 91 tailors, 8 trouser sewers, 7 linen weavers, 37 knitters, 13 artisans, and textile merchants returned to Prague. In 1724, among 3093 Jews who were in Bohemia, 182 were tailors.

In 1673, there were masters of 8 Jewish tailors in the Mikulov (Nilosburg) and each had a student and assistant. In 1713, there were 12 Jewish tailors as well as many others used to sell clothes in Prostejov. In the Thirty Year's War (1618-1648), thousand sets of uniforms of soldiers were transported.

The first textile factory in Europe was opened by Mayer Mandel (1820- 1888) in 1859. He was able to distribute his products from one factory to all Turkish Army and the Balkan states.

Jewish industrialists made Prostejov the centre of the modern textile industry in Czechoslovakia. In the 16th and 17th centuries, the Jews began to use art extensively in tailoring in Poland-Lithuania for the first time. The Jews helped the independent guilds for the work of creating and developing. But the Jews did not get involved in the job of applying their level and rank.

There were 74 Jewish weavers and tailors in Warsaw in the year 1865.

ENGLAND

As the cloth distributors Jews were the first to trade second-hand cloth with Britain in the 18th century. By the end of the 18th century, the number of Jews in Britain to distribute second-hand clothes had reached 1,000 - 1,500. By 1850, they were active distributors, numbering between 500 and 600. They used to sell whole clothes, and if they were torn, they would make waistcoats to distribute. At this time, they used to buy cheap and damaged clothes from the East India Company. East India Company established their authority mostly by selling cheap and torn clothes. The Jews also made a name for themselves in the trade of hats. They used to do both making and selling hats. As the community grew, the community leaders began to cut down the number of hawkers and apprentice Jewish youths, who were involved in tailoring, hat making, and shoemaking.

Therefore, by 1850, London developed a community of craftsmen of indigenous Jewish heritage. Along with this, they also developed middle class textile entrepreneurs, contractors and middlemen. A social revolution took place when even the daily wage earners could buy new clothes. The style or design of the new clothes looked like those worn by the rich, but the quality differed. Among two industries, one was Hymn which employed 6,000 employees and paid them 200,000 per annum and the other was E. Moses and Son which was very famous in advertising style. These two industries started a new development.

These two factories supplied cloth to the immigrants who migrated to the colonies. After the introduction of 'Singer' sewing machine in 1850 and 1860, there was a good motivation to meet the needs of these big companies. As the number of immigrants from Eastern Europe increased in about 1880, the number of Jews in tailoring decreased. According to the census of 1901, 40 out of 100 Russian-Polish immigrants and 50 out of 100 women got involved in the business of making shoes and slippers.

In Manchester, UK the immigrant Jews were in the business of making caps. The first development of water proofing was done by these immigrant Jews in Manchester. Working long hours in small and poorly-ventilated spaces made it very difficult for migrant workers to achieve perfection in their work.

Towards the beginning of the 20th century, Montague Burton produced a special type of bespoke tailoring for his customers to great effect and chained shops for retail distribution. In this process, he also promoted the role of Jews in the textile industry in terms of producing and distributing large results. A vivid example of this is the Marks and Spencer. Jews were also distributors for the large textile industry. They worked as retailers and also manufactured readymade clothes in huge numbers for women. Before 1939, Jewish women got involved in making dresses and tailoring, but in the middle of the 20th century, they started giving priority to the work of the office. For nearly two centuries, the Anglo-Jewry (Jews) were associated with the textile industry. Their roles also changed, from hawkers to retailers, operators to manufacturers, and merchants to street vendors.

THE UNITED STATES

Even before the 19th century, the Jews played a major role in the production of readymade clothes in Germany. German Jewish immigrants traded especially second-hand clothes in Europe. Many of them followed the same profession even after reaching America. After the Civil War, the demand for readymade clothes started to increase. Because, after the civil war, more people were living in the city than in former times. Cutting knife operated by machine also played a major role in producing many clothes in 1870. The distribution of second-hand clothes was done by the cloth merchants, many of whom were German Jews. Some of these people also started distributing readymade clothes.

After Eastern European Jews arrived in America, there was an immediate need for work and they began working in the textile industry. Many of them had the experience of tailoring before. Contractors used to hire new immigrants for little money and wages. So, they gave first priority to them. The contractor used to take the various works of textile finishing to the house. Because of this, children and everyone in the house worked even to earn a little money. Immigrant Jews from Eastern Europe went to America and gathered some experience as well as capital. They tried to establish themselves as employers in the textile industry. By the time of the First World War, Eastern European Jews had established themselves prominently as employers and contractors of the textile industry everywhere, because they could work with little capital invested in these areas. The Jews continued in this area until the year of 1970, and after that, the situation did not remain the same. There are many Jewish workers in the textile sector, but very few new Jewish workers have entered this sector. After this, there were very few Jewish workers in this area. After Jewish, Italian, African American, and Puerto Rican started to grow slowly in the American textile sector.

At the same time, ladies' garment was decentralized for cheap labour. The Jews continuously participated in the American industry until 1970.

IN ISRAEL

Tailoring and allied industries developed in Israel rapidly particularly for several reasons.

1. Due to the increase in population and their purchasing power, the local demand continuously increased.

2. Imports were banned by 1950 and 1960, which gave local builders a better opportunity to market.

3. Government's financial support for high-yield investments and certainty of prices, etc.

After 1960, many developments took place along with changes in the government's policy. Due to this, both inside and outside of the construction company changed. In other words, it can be called fashion and quality. Comparatively, within a few years, Israel has reached a good position in the world's fashion industry. Their good products are: swimsuits, beach wear, knits, women's underwear, sports clothes, raincoat, leather coat, etc.

Most of the Israel fashion clothing are made by Israeli fashion designers. Israel has managed to advance the world clothing centre in France, Italy, and the American continents.

Israel regularly participates in domestic and international fashion fair programs on a weekly basis. US, Germany, France and Scandinavia, the main exporting countries, have opened their sales centres. Fashion centres have been opened to increase the export and ensure the quality. By the year 2000, the export of fashion product clothing of Israel has reached $670 million annually.

The reason why it is difficult to tell the family name in Nepal and outside Nepal for centuries is mysterious. That's why I became curious to find out the secret and it would be impossible just by entering and staying in that community.

For centuries, my country, Nepal, has been very sick because of the caste system and untouchability. This disease is not only in one community but it is incurable in every community. That's why I am presenting caste system, family name and its reality to all my community after many years of hard work.

What do you call a garment maker who sews clothes in Nepal? If asked, you don't even have to teach a one-year-old child to say tailor (a Nepali caste of tailors). And if a small child of tailor is called into someone's house, it is said, "I am a child of a small caste and cannot go inside." It is a disease and a curse in that community since the mother's womb down from centuries.

Now let's see, how Adam, the first man of creation, made a garment to cover his shame, and private parts after realizing that he was naked after disobeying God.

"Then the eyes of both of them were opened, and they knew that they were naked; and they sewed fig leaves together and made themselves coverings." (Genesis 3:7).

Adam Damai, the father of all of us, and Eve Damini, made *daura suruwal* (tabard and trouser) and *chowbandi choli* (small blouse), sari (traditional lower dress for women) and wore them. "The son of Methuselah, the son of Enoch, the son of Jared, the son of Mahalalel, the son of Cainan" (Luke 3:37). Cainan was the son of Enoch; Enoch was the son of Seth; Seth was the son of Adam; and Adam was the son of God.

We do not know anything about how many days and months the father and mother of all human beings spent making and sewing clothes, but whether we all believe it or not, we cannot deny the truth. But tailor (Siojikar) means the one who goes forward in good deeds by playing the *damaha* (a type of large drum). tailor came from this damaha. tailor is called auspicious caste in Nepali society. When we seriously study the Bible passage below as well as by various evidences, we will get the answer to the question of why.

"Then, the Lord spoke to Moses, saying, 2 'See, I have called by name Bezalel the son of Uri, the son of Hur, of the tribe of Judah. 3 And I have filled him with the Spirit of God, in wisdom, in understanding, in knowledge, and in all manner of workmanship, 4 to design artistic works, to work in gold, in silver, in bronze, 5 in cutting jewels for setting, in carving wood, and to work in all manner of workmanship. 6 And I, indeed I, have appointed with him Aholiab the son of Ahisamach, of the tribe of Dan; and I have put wisdom in the hearts of all the gifted artisans, that they may make all that I have commanded you: 7 the tabernacle of meeting, the ark of the Testimony and the mercy seat that is on it, and all the furniture of the tabernacle—8 the table and its utensils, the pure gold lampstand with all its utensils, the altar of incense, 9 the altar of burnt offering with all its utensils, and the laver and its base—10 the garments of ministry, the holy garments for Aaron the priest and the garments of his sons, to minister as priests, 11 and the anointing oil and sweet incense for the holy place. According to all that I have commanded you they shall do.'" (Exodus 31:1-11).

"30 And Moses said to the children of Israel, 'See, the Lord has called by name Bezalel the son of Uri, the son of Hur, of the tribe of Judah; 31 and He has filled him with the Spirit of God, in wisdom and understanding, in knowledge and all manner of workmanship, 32 to design artistic works, to work in gold and silver and bronze, 33 in cutting jewels for setting, in carving wood, and to work in all manner of artistic workmanship.34 And He has put in his heart the ability to teach, in him and Aholiab the son of Ahisamach, of the tribe of Dan. 35 He has filled them with skill to do all manner of work of the engraver and the designer and the tapestry maker, in blue, purple, and scarlet thread, and fine linen, and of the weaver—those who do every work and those who design artistic works.'"(Exodus 35:30-35).

God has already given us the ability to do temple work. I mean most of these community worshipers in Nepal are gifted and proficient in music. We find written evidence in the Bible about the daily behaviour of these communities and the religious laws and regulations during the special festivals of Nepal. The tailor are called tail-eaters. How did this happen?

Let's see the Biblical passage, "Likewise, this is the law of the trespass offering (it is most holy): 2 In the place where they kill the burnt offering, they shall kill the trespass offering. And its blood he shall sprinkle all around on the altar. 3 And he shall offer from it all its fat. The fat tail and the fat that covers the entrails, 4 the two kidneys and the fat that is on them by the flanks, and the fatty lobe attached to the liver above the kidneys, he shall remove; 5 and the priest shall burn them on the altar as an offering made by fire to the Lord. It is a trespass offering. 6 Every male among the priests may eat it. It shall be eaten in a holy place. It is most holy." (Leviticus 7:1-6).

After performing any sacrifice either one has to deliver it to tailor or he comes to collect it himself.

We have a custom that this tail is separated by all castes of both Brahmin and Mongolian communities for Damai.

In the season in which the First fruit grows, the first part of it should be distributed to Damai. There is a custom of eating *Nwagi* (first fruits) in Nepal.

"28 It shall be, in regard to their inheritance, that I am their inheritance. You shall give them no possession in Israel, for I am their possession. 29 They shall eat the grain offering, the sin offering, and the trespass offering; every dedicated thing in Israel shall be theirs. 30 The best of all first fruits of any kind, and every sacrifice of any kind from all your sacrifices, shall be the priest's; also, you shall give to the priest the first of your ground meal, to cause a blessing to rest on your house. 31 The priests shall not eat anything, bird or beast, that died naturally or was torn by wild beasts." (Ezekiel 44:28-31).

"And the Lord spoke to Moses" (Leviticus 23:9).

A CUSTOM OF PLAYING NARSINGA (HORN CURVED IN SHAPE) AND BLOWING TRUMPET

"Then they took an oath before the Lord with a loud voice, with shouting and trumpets and rams' horns" (2 Chronicles 15:14).

"And the Lord spoke to Moses, saying: 2 'Make two silver trumpets for yourself; you shall make them of hammered work; you shall use them for calling the congregation and for directing the movement of the camps. 3When they blow both of them, all the congregation shall gather before you at the door of the tabernacle of meeting. 4 But if they blow only one, then the leaders, the heads of the divisions of Israel, shall gather to you. 5 When you sound the advance, the camps that lie on the east side shall then begin their journey. 6When you sound the advance the second time, then the camps that lie on the south side shall begin their journey; they shall sound the call for them to begin their journeys. 7 And when the assembly is to be gathered together, you shall blow, but not sound the advance. 8 The sons of Aaron, the priests, shall blow the trumpets; and these shall be to you as an ordinance forever throughout your generations. 9 When you go to war in your land against the enemy who oppresses you, then you shall sound an alarm with the trumpets, and you will be remembered before the Lord your God, and you will be saved from your enemies. 10 Also in the day of your gladness, in your appointed feasts, and at the beginning of your months, you shall blow the trumpets over your burnt offerings and over the sacrifices of your peace offerings; and they shall be a memorial for you before your God: I am the Lord your God" (Numbers 10:1-10).

'Nar' means man in Sanskrit language and Singh means power. tailor community has been doing this work of showing the power of masculinity since the beginning of history in Nepal. It was also customary to blow the trumpet during the coronation of the king.

33The king also said to them, "Take with you the servants of your lord, and have Solomon my son ride on my own mule, and take him down to Gihon. 34 There let Zadok the priest and Nathan the prophet anoint him king over Israel; and blow the horn, and say, 'Long live King Solomon!' 35 Then, you shall come up after him, and he shall come and sit on my throne, and he shall be king in my place. For I have appointed him to be ruler over Israel and Judah." 36 Benaiah the son of Jehoiada answered the king and said, "Amen! May the Lord God of my lord the king say so too. 37 As the Lord has been with my lord the king, even so may He be with Solomon, and make his throne greater than the throne of my lord King David."38 So Zadok the priest, Nathan the prophet, Benaiah the son of Jehoiada, the Cherethites, and the Pelethites went down and had Solomon ride on King David's mule, and took him to Gihon. 39Then, Zadok the priest took a horn of oil from the tabernacle and anointed Solomon. And they blew the horn, and all the people said, "Long live King Solomon!" 40 And all the people went up after him; and the people played the flutes and rejoiced with great joy, so that the earth seemed to split with their sound. (1 Kings 1:33-40)

It is customary to play Narasinha, Sanahi, Damaha and other instruments in almost all auspicious activities like dedicating a temple.

Damai are not allowed to blow the conch shell and tailor have not blown the conch shell in any auspicious work. Perhaps, it is possible to show the shrine or some kind of society that we are Hindus less than you. But this attempt to show equality in society by being fake is not true.

Earlier in the past, it was customary to give a separate vacancy quota to tailor people in the army and police for sewing clothes and playing fiddles and other instruments.

When going to the bride's house with the bridegroom at the wedding, this is how the custom of keeping out the tailor people who play *panchebaja* (five instruments) started.

27 Now, at the dedication of the wall of Jerusalem they sought out the Levites in all their places, to bring them to Jerusalem to celebrate the dedication with gladness, both with thanksgivings and singing, with cymbals and stringed instruments and harps. 28 And the sons of the singers gathered together from the countryside around Jerusalem, from the villages of the Netophathites, 29from the house of Gilgal, and from the fields of Geba and Azmaveth; for the singers had built themselves villages all around Jerusalem. 30 Then the priests and Levites purified themselves, and purified the people, the gates, and the wall. 31 So I brought the leaders of Judah up on the wall, and appointed two large thanksgiving choirs. One went to the right hand on the wall toward the Refuse Gate. 32 After them went Hoshaiah and half of the leaders of Judah, 33 and Azariah, Ezra, Meshullam, 34 Judah, Benjamin, Shemaiah, Jeremiah, 35 and some of the priests' sons with trumpets—Zechariah the son of Jonathan, the son of Shemaiah, the son of Mattaniah, the son of Michaiah, the son of Zaccur, the son of Asaph, 36 and his brethren, Shemaiah, Azarel, Milalai, Gilalai, Maai, Nethanel, Judah, and Hanani, with the musical instruments of David the man of God. And Ezra the scribe went before them. 37 By the Fountain Gate, in front of them, they went up the stairs of the City of David, on the stairway of the wall, beyond the house of David, as far as the Water Gate eastward.38 The other thanksgiving choir went the opposite way, and I was behind them with half of the people on the wall, going past the Tower of the Ovens as far as the Broad Wall, 39 and above the Gate of Ephraim, above the Old Gate, above the Fish Gate, the Tower of Hananel, the Tower of the Hundred, as far as the Sheep Gate; and they stopped by the Gate of the Prison. 40 So the two thanksgiving choirs stood in the house of God, likewise I and the half of the rulers with me; 41 and the priests, Eliakim, Maaseiah, Minjamin, Michaiah, Elioenai, Zechariah, and Hananiah, with trumpets; 42 also Maaseiah, Shemaiah, Eleazar, Uzzi, Jehohanan, Malchijah, Elam, and Ezer. The singers sang loudly with Jezrahiah the director. 43Also that day they offered great sacrifices, and rejoiced, for God had made them rejoice with great joy; the women and the children

also rejoiced, so that the joy of Jerusalem was heard afar off. 44 And at the same time, some were appointed over the rooms of the storehouse for the offerings, the first fruits, and the tithes, to gather into them from the fields of the cities the portions specified by the Law for the priests and Levites; for Judah rejoiced over the priests and Levites who ministered. 45 Both the singers and the gatekeepers kept the charge of their God and the charge of the purification, according to the command of David and Solomon his son. 46 For in the days of David and Asaph of old there were chiefs of the singers, and songs of praise and thanksgiving to God. 47 In the days of Zerubbabel and in the days of Nehemiah all Israel gave the portions for the singers and the gatekeepers, a portion for each day. They also consecrated holy things for the Levites, and the Levites consecrated them for the children of Aaron. (Nehemiah 12:27-47)

The tailor community is forbidden to touch the corpse if a person of another community dies, and in various regions, the tailor people are forbidden to go to a funeral procession.

"They shall not defile themselves by coming near a dead person. Only for father or mother, for son or daughter, for brother or unmarried sister may they defile themselves." (Ezekiel 44:25)

There is a tradition of making a shrine in the house of some tailor community, and at different times, the priests of their own community of tailor come, and before the worship starts, make a hexagonal figure map of the Star of David and line it with rice flour. But the tailor community is forbidden to prove that they are Hindus in other societies and make agreements by worshiping idols.

"14 Nevertheless they would not hear, but stiffened their necks, like the necks of their fathers, who did not believe in the Lord their God. 15 And they rejected His statutes and His covenant that He had made with their fathers, and His testimonies which He had testified against them; they followed idols, became idolaters, and went after the nations who were all around them, concerning whom the Lord had charged them that they should not do like them." (2 Kings 17:14-15)

For hundreds of years, almost all communities have land in Nepal, but especially when we study deeply, we find that we experience very interesting and mysterious customs. It is customary to give tail portions during *Chaite Dashain*, Kartik or *Mansire Dashain*, also during Tihar, *Mansire Poornima*, *Maghe Sakranti* and *Bhimsen* Puja (various mini festivals for expiating one's sins) and their portion should be kept separately on various *Aunshi Poornima* and other festivals. There is a custom of giving *radi* (woolen mattress), sheep, and lambs once a year from the herd to the mountains. This is especially the case if one's son gets married.

"The priests, the Levites—all the tribe of Levi—shall have no part nor inheritance with Israel; they shall eat the offerings of the Lord made by fire, and His portion. 2 Therefore, they shall have no inheritance among their brethren; the Lord is their inheritance, as He said to them. 3 And this shall be the priest's due from the people, from those who offer a sacrifice, whether it is bull or sheep: they shall give to the priest the shoulder, the cheeks, and the stomach. 4 The first fruits of your grain and your new wine and your oil, and the first of the fleece of your sheep, you shall give him. 5 For the Lord your God has chosen him out of all your tribes to stand to minister in the name of the Lord, him and his sons forever" (Deuteronomy 18:1-5).

There is a tradition or custom that tailor must be given the first-fruit portion, of the first morsel on auspicious deed of marriage. They don't play instruments if they are not given the portions.

David built houses for himself in the City of David; and he prepared a place for the ark of God, and pitched a tent for it. 2 Then David said, "No one may carry the ark of God but the Levites, for the Lord has chosen them to carry the ark of God and to minister before Him forever." 3 And David gathered all Israel together at Jerusalem, to bring up the ark of the Lord to its place, which he had prepared for it. 4 Then, David assembled the children of Aaron and the Levites: 5 of the sons of Kohath, Uriel the chief, and one hundred and twenty of his brethren; 6 of the sons of Merari, Asaiah the chief, and two hundred and twenty of his brethren; 7 of the sons of Gershom, Joel the chief, and one hundred and thirty of his brethren; 8 of the sons of Elizaphan, Shemaiah the chief, and two hundred of his brethren; 9 of the sons of Hebron, Eliel the chief, and eighty of his brethren; 10 of the sons of Uzziel, Amminadab the chief, and one hundred and twelve of his brethren. 11 And David called for Zadok and Abiathar the priests, and for the Levites: for Uriel, Asaiah, Joel, Shemaiah, Eliel, and Amminadab. 12 He said to them, "You are the heads of the fathers' houses of the Levites; sanctify yourselves, you and your brethren, that you may bring up the ark of the Lord God of Israel to the place I have prepared for it. 13 For because you did not do it the first time, the Lord our God broke out against us, because we did not consult Him about the proper order." 14 So the priests and the Levites sanctified themselves to bring up the ark of the Lord God of Israel. 15 And the children of the Levites bore the ark of God on their shoulders, by its poles, as Moses had commanded according to the word of the Lord.

16 Then, David spoke to the leaders of the Levites to appoint their brethren to be the singers accompanied by instruments of music, stringed instruments, harps, and cymbals, by raising the voice with resounding joy. 17 So the Levites appointed Heman the son of Joel; and of his brethren, Asaph the son of Berechiah; and of their brethren, the sons of Merari, Ethan the son of Kushaiah; 18 and with them their brethren of the second rank: Zechariah, Ben, Jaaziel, Shemiramoth, Jehiel, Unni, Eliab, Benaiah, Maaseiah, Mattithiah, Elipheleh, Mikneiah, Obed-Edom, and Jeiel, the gatekeepers; 19 the singers, Heman, Asaph, and Ethan, were to sound the cymbals of bronze; 20 Zechariah, Aziel, Shemiramoth, Jehiel, Unni, Eliab, Maaseiah, and Benaiah, with strings according to Alamoth; 21Mattithiah, Elipheleh, Mikneiah, Obed-Edom, Jeiel, and Azaziah, to direct with harps on the Sheminith; 22 Chenaniah, leader of the Levites, was instructor in charge of the music, because he was skillful; 23 Berechiah and Elkanah were doorkeepers for the ark; 24 Shebaniah, Joshaphat, Nethanel, Amasai, Zechariah, Benaiah, and Eliezer, the priests, were to blow the trumpets before the ark of God; and Obed-Edom and Jehiah, doorkeepers for the ark. 25So David, the

elders of Israel, and the captains over thousands went to bring up the ark of the covenant of the Lord from the house of Obed-Edom with joy. 26 And so it was, when God helped the Levites who bore the ark of the covenant of the Lord, that they offered seven bulls and seven rams. 27 David was clothed with a robe of fine linen, as were all the Levites who bore the ark, the singers, and Chenaniah the music master with the singers. David also wore a linen ephod. 28 Thus, all Israel brought up the ark of the covenant of the Lord with shouting and with the sound of the horn, with trumpets and with cymbals, making music with stringed instruments and harps.29 And it happened, as the ark of the covenant of the Lord came to the City of David, that Michal, Saul's daughter, looked through a window and saw King David whirling and playing music; and she despised him in her heart. (1 Chronicles 15:1-29)

"So they brought the ark of God, and set it in the midst of the tabernacle that David had erected for it. Then, they offered burnt offerings and peace offerings before God. 2 And when David had finished offering the burnt offerings and the peace offerings, he blessed the people in the name of the Lord. 3 Then, he distributed to everyone of Israel, both man and woman, to everyone a loaf of bread, a piece of meat, and a cake of raisins. 4 And he appointed some of the Levites to minister before the ark of the Lord, to commemorate, to thank, and to praise the Lord God of Israel: 5 Asaph the chief, and next to him Zechariah, then Jeiel, Shemiramoth, Jehiel, Mattithiah, Eliab, Benaiah, and Obed Edom: Jeiel with stringed instruments and harps, but Asaph made music with cymbals; 6 Benaiah and Jahaziel the priests regularly blew the trumpets before the ark of the covenant of God." (1 Chronicles 16:1-6)

The first use of the Hebrew word tailor, to make clothes, to sew, is found in the Hebrew literature like Mishanaik and Midrashim. There are frequent mentions about clothes making people in Talmud as well. There is also a custom of addressing him as Talmud Saheb. (shab 1:3, 11Bk 10:10)

During those times, Jews used to make clothes in Muslim countries, sometimes in small numbers. Almost every Jewish community needed people to make their own clothes. They had to be based on religious laws and involved and follow religious laws and the presence of a Jewish cloth maker in auspicious work was mandatory. The church also encouraged to wear special clothing, and all communities were willing.

Tailoring was understood as giving money as a bond for good repair because a guarantee of goods and clothes had to be kept for good repair. In Muslim countries, the church did not behave like that. This means that there was no practice of pledging money and clothing.

The small and medium level of tailoring had a lot of importance in the Jewish society and it also played an important role.

All worked as weavers and tailors in the Jewish village of Aven until 1948 (S.D Goitein, In: Jsos,17 (1954), 3-26). The Jewish tailors were troubled by guilds in Central Europe. And they used to hinder the sewing of special and distinct clothes for the Jews.

Second-hand goods and old clothes were repaired and put up for sale in Italy and especially in Rome. Jewish tailors were seen in the profession and work of tailoring clothes since the fifteenth century. A quarter or a half of Jewish tailors seem to be involved in the cloth trade business in various parts of the world in the 16th century.

BERNARDINO RAMAZZINI (1633-1714)

He was the first authority to study occupational disease which was caused by various dust and dirt when old clothes were thrown away. He said that many Jews had weak eyes, legs and lungs.

The main reason for all this is that the house has little light and narrow windows, so the air is low and old clothes are made in such a place. Doing so has affected their health. In Central Europe, as elsewhere, Jewish tailoring was bound by the laws of the *shaatnez*. It was related to repairing and selling old clothes. There was a great difference of opinion between the Christians and the Jewish guilds in Prague because of the accusations of illegally selling new clothes to the Jewish tailors.

Due to this dispute, the Prague community was expelled in the year 1745. The expelled Jews went from village to village and started producing cloth, so that no one came to buy new cloth in Prague. Due to this situation, the Christian tailors also were affected.

In 1418, among the Jewish families, 91 tailors, 8 trouser sewers, 7 linen weavers, 37 knitters, 13 artisans, and textile merchants returned to Prague. In 1724, among 3093 Jews who were in Bohemia 182 were tailors.

In 1859, Mayer Mandell (1820-1888) opened the first textile factory in Europe.

In 1673, there were masters of 8 Jewish tailors in the Mikulov (Nilosburg) and each had a student and assistant.

In 1713, there were 12 Jewish tailors as well as many others used to sell clothes in Prostejov. In the Thirty Year's War (1618-1648) thousand sets of uniforms of soldiers were transported.

He was able to distribute his products from one factory to all Turkish Army and Balkan states. Jewish industrialists made Prostejov the center of the modern textile industry in Czechoslovakia.

In the 16th and 17th centuries, the Jews began to use art extensively in tailoring in Poland-Lithuania for the first time. For this, Jewish tailors developed independent, shoe stuffing, embroidering, gold and silver ribbons, and embellishing the edges of metals.

There were 74 Jewish weavers and tailors in Warsaw in the year 1795.

As the cloth distributors, Jews were the first to trade second-hand cloth with Britain in the 18th century.

By the end of the 18ᵗʰ century, the number of Jews in Britain to distribute second-hand clothes had reached 1,000-1,500. By 1850, they were active distributors, numbering between 500 and 600.

They used to make whole clothes or if they were torn, they would make other types of clothes, bags, toys, materials and sell them. During this time, they used to buy cheap and torn clothes from the India's company. India's company established their authority mostly by selling cheap and torn clothes. In Nepal, there is also a custom of insulting tailor as a community that patches of the knees of pantaloons.

Jews also sewed hats and brought the custom of wearing hats to different parts of the world. There are nearly 16 Jewish orthodox groups. Each group is clearly identified from the shape of their hats.

In Russia as well as in other Catholic countries it can be assumed that the custom of hats worn by priests and bishops started with the Jews.

The Jews also made a name for themselves in the trade of hats. We Nepalese carry the symbol of Mount Everest on our hats and brandish it and sing proudly. This cap which we Nepalese wear as national dress, similar cap is worn by Turkish people as well as countries where Jews live. It is also found in various countries including Iran, Iraq, Ethiopia, and Armenia. Of course, now modern designers have made their own by making different shapes, but the sources prove that the beginning was from Jewish tailors.

As the trade and skills of these Jewish communities increased, the community officials used to sew hats, make shoes and sell them door to door.

As the community grew, the community leaders began to cut down the number of apprenticed Jewish youths. Therefore, by 1850, London developed a community of craftsmen who were indigenously Jewish. Along with this, they also developed middle class textile entrepreneurs, contractors and middlemen. The style or design of the new clothes looked like those worn by the rich, but the quality differed.

Among two industries one was Hymn which employed 6,000 employees and paid them 200,000 per annum and the other was E. Moses and Son which was very famous in advertising style. These two industries started a new development.

These two industries supplied cloth to the immigrants who migrated to the colonies. After the introduction of 'Singer' sewing machine in 1850 and in 1860, there was a good motivation to meet the needs of these big companies. As the number of immigrants from Eastern Europe increased in about 1880, the number of Jews in tailoring decreased.

According to the census of 1901, 40 out of 100 Russian-Polish immigrants and 50 out of 100 women got involved in the business of making shoes and slippers.

In Manchester and London, the immigrant Jews were in the business of making caps. The first development of waterproofing was done by these immigrant Jews in Manchester.

Making hats and waterproofing factories superseded technologically superior rainproof garments. The immigrant tailor had no effect on the bespoke trade in London supplied.

The Jews also developed factories for making readymade clothes at home and in companies, large wholesale clothes, women's jackets, long coats of gold chain, gold and silver wooden bottoms, stitches, various jewellery and decorative items made of bones and leather. Most Jewish women were proficient in this, as Lydia was a woman who sewed clothes and sold them in the market. But later, she started holding high-level offices and responsibilities at different levels.

"Now a certain woman named Lydia heard us. She was a seller of purple from the city of Thyatira, who worshiped God. The Lord opened her heart to heed the things spoken by Paul." (Acts 16:14)

Some are still working in the same business.

THE UNITED STATES

Before 1980, the Jews in Germany played a major role in the readymade production by sewing clothes at home as well as producing clothes at home.

German Jewish immigrants traded especially second-hand clothes in Europe.

Many Jews later came to America and adopted the profession of sewing the same clothes, preparing them at home, and taking them to the market. After the civil war, there were more people living in the city.

Cutting knife operated by machine also played a major role in producing many clothes in 1870.

The distribution of second-hand clothes was done by the cloth merchants and many of whom were German Jews.

After Eastern European Jews arrived in America, there was an immediate need for work and they began working in the textile industry. Because many of them had the experience of tailoring before. Because their profession was hereditary, there was no need to continue learning.

Contractors used to hire new immigrants for little money and wages. That is why the contractors gave the job of tailoring to the Jews.

Immigrant Jews from Eastern Europe went to America and gathered some experience as well as capital. They tried to establish themselves as employers in the textile industry.

By World War I, former European Jews had established themselves prominently everywhere as employers and contractors in the textile industry. Because these areas could be worked with a little capital investment.

Until 1970, the presence of Jews in this area continued, and after that, the situation was no longer the same, and many workers in the textile industry remained exclusively Jewish. New Jewish youth joined. After that, there were very few Jews working in this area.

After the Jews, the American Jews advanced in this area and it is known that the Jews were very gifted and proficient in the profession of making clothes and sewing, and later, the name of the jeans paint and the jacket was also named Levis' origin because it originated from the family of Levi, the descendants of Levi, the descendants of the priests. It comes to hear that it is named Levi's Jeans.

In America, as well as in the world, the big agencies like FBI and companies like the Coca Cola have Jews in various leading positions and controlling powers. And even though America is a very big country and the people of Israel, a small country, have a great role. To tell the truth, it is the job of the Jews to keep America safe and to take it to a mighty height. But when we hear from the news, we hear the opposite news that it is America that protects Israel. But because the real Jews are the children of the Holy God who live in fear and fear of God, they either kill or exterminate the Jews or they respect the Jews as a source of blessings and knowledge and science. That is what we are witnessing now.

Looking at the history of America, a country discovered by a European a few centuries ago, where the Red Indians had their own customs and traditions and they were ancestor and nature worshipers. Later, because of the prayers and teachings of the Jewish Christians, the God-fearing presidents made covenants in the country according to the word of God and mentioned the verses of the Bible. In a short period of time, the speed of development of the country of Jews and Christians has reached and the place that America has reached is probably rare.

It is important for all of us to know the God who blesses America. And at the present time, the Jews' occupation and migration, moving from one country to another, and the beginning of the tailoring profession in Nepal, was explained by someone from India. He overlooked forefathers and whirled us in confusion and wounded us further. As suggested the information above, the tailoring profession of Jews in Nepal is based on the Bible and there is nothing to disprove that the forefathers of the communities involved in jewellery metal and leather profession are not Jews. Let us try to understand well the various rules and professions of the 80 per cent of Nepal's festivals and living communities and start developing.

LOOK AT THE SOURCE

Later, the whole family of Jewish tailors even small children, in Italy, Africa, Puerto Rico, and other countries of the world, have been doing the work of sewing clothes, jewellery, and making various leather goods. The tailoring industry developed rapidly in Israel due to a number of reasons, and continued growth in the local area due to population growth and their purchasing power.

By the 1950 and 1960, import bans provided good opportunities for local manufacturers to market. The government's financial and investment support for large-scale investment and price certainty guarantee wholesale price, etc.

After 1960, many developments took place along with changes in government policy. This led to changes both outside and inside the construction company. In other words, it can be called fashion and quality. Comparatively, within a few years, Israel managed to occupy a good position in the world's fashion industry. These are their best products: swimsuits, beach wear, women's indoor and outdoor wear, sports clothes, and all waterproof items.

Most Israeli fashion dresses are made by Israeli fashion designers. Israel has succeeded in advancing the world clothing centre in France, Italy, and in the American continents.

Israel regularly participates in weekly domestic and international fashion fairs.

The main export countries are America, Germany, France, and Scandinavia. In various countries, not only selling fashion clothes but also the complete fashion jewellery, shoes, and leather bag material centres have been opened. Fashion centres have been opened to increase exports and ensure quality.

By the year 2000, Israel's fashion apparel exports reached US $670 million annually. Then, the Lord spoke to Moses, saying: 2 "See, I have called by name Bezalel the son of Uri, the son of Hur, of the tribe of Judah. 3 And I have filled him with the Spirit of God, in wisdom, in understanding, in knowledge, and in all manner of workmanship, 4 to design artistic works, to work in gold, in silver, in bronze, 5 in cutting jewels for setting, in carving wood, and to work in all manner of workmanship. 6 "And I, indeed I, have appointed with him Aholiab the son of Ahisamach, of the tribe of Dan; and I have put wisdom in the hearts of all the gifted artisans, that they may make all that I have commanded you: 7 the tabernacle of meeting, the ark of the Testimony and the mercy seat that is on it, and all the furniture of the tabernacle— 8 the table and its utensils, the pure gold lampstand with all its utensils, the altar of incense, 9 the altar of burnt offering with all its utensils, and the laver and its base— 10 the garments of ministry, the holy garments for Aaron the priest and the garments of his sons, to minister as priests, 11 and the anointing oil and sweet incense for the holy place. According to all that I have commanded you they shall do." (Exodus 31:1-11)

"30 And Moses said to the children of Israel, 'See, the Lord has called by name Bezalel the son of Uri, the son of Hur, of the tribe of Judah; 31 and He has filled him with the Spirit of God, in wisdom and understanding, in knowledge and all manner of workmanship, 32 to design artistic works, to work in gold and silver and bronze, 33 in cutting jewels for setting, in carving wood, and to work in all manner of artistic workmanship.34 And He has put in his heart the ability to teach, in him and Aholiab the son of Ahisamach, of the tribe of Dan. 35 He has filled them with skill to do all manner of work of the engraver and the designer and the tapestry maker, in blue, purple, and scarlet thread, and fine linen, and of the weaver—those who do every work and those who design artistic works.'" (Exodus 35:30-35)

The strong foundation of God for these craftsmen is that all the work they have to do is filled with God's efficiency. These communities are the anointed communities who have been given especially the temple responsibility.

Vishwakarma in India means you can hold the world in your fist. The karma of the world is in the hands of these communities. It can destroy the world by making bombs and shells. That is why the title of Vishwakarma has been given to worship as a god. In Nepal, these communities are also forbidden to touch the corpse.

"They shall not defile themselves by coming near a dead person. Only for father or mother, for son or daughter, for brother or unmarried sister may they defile themselves." (Ezekiel 44:25).

"Behold, I have created the blacksmith who blows the coals in the fire, who brings forth an instrument for his work; and I have created the spoiler to destroy. No weapon formed against you shall prosper, and every tongue which rises against you in judgment you shall condemn. This is the heritage of the servants of the Lord, and their righteousness is from me," says the Lord. (Isaiah 54:16-17) Behold, I have created the blacksmith who blows the coals in the fire, who brings forth an instrument for his work.

In the context of Nepal, even though they are nicknamed Dalits, they make idols but do not worship them. In these communities too, there is a tradition of putting the Star of David on the rice flour for auspicious work. Like other communities, these communities also do not like to intermarry with other communities.

- A community of coppersmiths who wrote the Bible on dead metal.

- There is evidence that some of the above surnames were taken by our Arya Pundits and kept by them. Therefore, there is confusion as to who is called a Dalit based on caste and who is called a worshiper of nature.

Although untouchability and caste systems seem to be similar in Nepal and India, there are many differences when studying this matter in depth. Where and how did the community known as special craftsmen in Nepal start?

Then, Moses gathered all the congregation of the children of Israel together, and said to them, "These are the words which the Lord has commanded you to do: 2 Work shall be done for six days, but the seventh day shall be a holy day for you, a Sabbath of rest to the Lord. Whoever does any work on it shall be put to death. 3 You shall kindle no fire throughout your dwellings on the Sabbath day."

4 And Moses spoke to all the congregation of the children of Israel, saying, "This is the thing which the Lord commanded, saying: 5 'Take from among you an offering to the Lord. Whoever is of a willing heart, let him bring it as an offering to the Lord: gold, silver, and bronze; 6 blue, purple, and scarlet thread, fine linen, and goats' hair; 7 ram skins dyed red, badger skins, and acacia wood; 8 oil for the light, and spices for the anointing oil and for the sweet incense; 9 onyx stones, and stones to be set in the ephod and in the breastplate.

10 'All who are gifted artisans among you shall come and make all that the Lord has commanded: 11 the tabernacle, its tent, its covering, its clasps, its boards, its bars, its pillars, and its sockets; 12 the ark and its poles, with the mercy seat, and the veil of the covering; 13 the table and its poles, all its utensils, and the showbread; 14 also the lampstand for the light, its utensils, its lamps, and the oil for the light; 15 the incense altar, its poles, the anointing oil, the sweet incense, and the screen for the door at the entrance of the tabernacle; 16 the altar of burnt offering with its bronze grating, its poles, all its utensils, and the laver and its base; 17 the hangings of the court, its pillars, their sockets, and the screen for the gate of the court; 18 the pegs of the tabernacle, the pegs of the court, and their cords; 19 the garments of ministry, for ministering in the holy place—the holy garments for Aaron the priest and the garments of his sons, to minister as priests.'"

20 And all the congregation of the children of Israel departed from the presence of Moses. 21 Then everyone came whose heart was stirred,

and everyone whose spirit was willing, and they brought the Lord's offering for the work of the tabernacle of meeting, for all its service, and for the holy garments. 22 They came, both men and women, as many as had a willing heart, and brought earrings and nose rings, rings and necklaces, all jewellery of gold, that is, every man who made an offering of gold to the Lord. 23 And every man, with whom was found blue, purple, and scarlet thread, fine linen, and goats' hair, red skins of rams, and badger skins, brought them. 24 Everyone who offered an offering of silver or bronze brought the Lord's offering. And everyone with whom was found acacia wood for any work of the service, brought it. 25 All the women who were gifted artisans spun yarn with their hands, and brought what they had spun, of blue, purple, and scarlet, and fine linen. 26 And all the women whose hearts stirred with wisdom spun yarn of goats' hair. 27 The rulers brought onyx stones, and the stones to be set in the ephod and in the breastplate, 28 and spices and oil for the light, for the anointing oil, and for the sweet incense. 29 The children of Israel brought a freewill offering to the Lord, all the men and women whose hearts were willing to bring material for all kinds of work which the Lord, by the hand of Moses, had commanded to be done. 30 And Moses said to the children of Israel, "See, the Lord has called by name Bezalel the son of Uri, the son of Hur, of the tribe of Judah; 31 and He has filled him with the Spirit of God, in wisdom and understanding, in knowledge and all manner of workmanship, 32 to design artistic works, to work in gold and silver and bronze, 33 in cutting jewels for setting, in carving wood, and to work in all manner of artistic workmanship.

34 "And He has put in his heart the ability to teach, in him and Aholiab the son of Ahisamach, of the tribe of Dan. 35 He has filled them with skill to do all manner of work of the engraver and the designer and the tapestry maker, in blue, purple, and scarlet thread, and fine linen, and of the weaver—those who do every work and those who design artistic works. (Exodus 35)

The communities endowed with skill and gift for materials of tabernacle were Damai, Kami, Saraki. As we begin to study about craftsman we see that they were

1. A community with skills who were given to make the equipment and materials of the temple.

2. The king's crown, throne and all the vessels, ornaments and all the instruments played by the Damais in auspicious work are also made by these artisans. They don't learn it. It is a community that has received blessings from God since the beginning. The blessing of the Lord runs in this family. Diamonds, pearls, gold, and silver are all made by this community.

But Solomon took thirteen years to build his own house; so, he finished all his house.

2 He also built the House of the Forest of Lebanon; its length was one hundred cubits, its width fifty cubits, and its height thirty cubits, with four rows of cedar pillars, and cedar beams on the pillars. 3And it was panelled with cedar above the beams that were on forty

five pillars, fifteen to a row. 4 There were windows with bevelled frames in three rows, and window was opposite window in three tiers. 5 And all the doorways and doorposts had rectangular frames; and window was opposite window in three tiers. 6 He also made the Hall of Pillars: its length was fifty cubits, and its width thirty cubits; and in front of them was a portico with pillars, and a canopy was in front of them.

7 Then, he made a hall for the throne, the Hall of Judgment, where he might judge; and it was panelled with cedar from floor to ceiling.

8 And the house where he dwelt had another court inside the hall, of like workmanship. Solomon also made a house like this hall for Pharaoh's daughter, whom he had taken as wife.

9 All these were of costly stones cut to size, trimmed with saws, inside and out, from the foundation to the eaves, and also on the outside to the great court. 10 The foundation was of costly stones, large stones,

some ten cubits and some eight cubits. 11And above were costly stones, hewn to size, and cedar wood. 12 The great court was enclosed with three rows of hewn stones and a row of cedar beams. So were the inner court of the house of the Lord and the vestibule of the temple.

13 Now King Solomon sent and brought Huram from Tyre. 14 He was the son of a widow from the tribe of Naphtali, and his father was a man of Tyre, a bronze worker; he was filled with wisdom and understanding and skill in working with all kinds of bronze work. So, he came to King Solomon and did all his work.

15 And he cast two pillars of bronze, each one eighteen cubits high, and a line of twelve cubits measured the circumference of each. 16 Then, he made two capitals of cast bronze, to set on the tops of the pillars. The height of one capital was five cubits, and the height of the other capital was five cubits. 17 He made a lattice network, with wreaths of chainwork, for the capitals which were on top of the pillars: seven chains for one capital and seven for the other capital. 18 So, he made the pillars, and two rows of pomegranates above the network all around to cover the capitals that were on top; and thus, he did for the other capital.

19 The capitals which were on top of the pillars in the hall were in the shape of lilies, four cubits. 20 The capitals on the two pillars also had pomegranates above, by the convex surface which was next to the network; and there were two hundred such pomegranates in rows on each of the capitals all around.

21 Then, he set up the pillars by the vestibule of the temple; he set up the pillar on the right and called its name Jachin, and he set up the pillar on the left and called its name Boaz. 22 The tops of the pillars were in the shape of lilies. So, the work of the pillars was finished.

23And he made the Sea of cast bronze, ten cubits from one brim to the other; it was completely round. Its height was five cubits, and a line of thirty cubits measured its circumference.

24 Below its brim were ornamental buds encircling it all around, ten to a cubit, all the way around the Sea. The ornamental buds were cast in two rows when it was cast. 25 It stood on twelve oxen: three looking toward the north, three looking toward the west, three looking toward the south, and three looking toward the east; the Sea was set upon them, and all their back parts pointed inward. 26 It was a handbreadth thick; and its brim was shaped like the brim of a cup, like a lily blossom. It contained two thousand baths.

27 He also made ten carts of bronze; four cubits was the length of each cart, four cubits its width, and three cubits its height. 28And this was the design of the carts: They had panels, and the panels were between frames; 29 on the panels that were between the frames were lions, oxen, and cherubim. And on the frames was a pedestal on top. Below the lions and oxen were wreaths of plaited work. 30 Every cart had four bronze wheels and axles of bronze, and its four feet had supports. Under the laver were supports of cast bronze beside each wreath. 31 Its opening inside the crown at the top was one cubit in diameter; and the opening was round, shaped like a pedestal, one and a half cubits in outside diameter; and also on the opening were engravings, but the panels were square, not round. 32 Under the panels were the four wheels, and the axles of the wheels were joined to the cart. The height of a wheel was one and a half cubits. 33 The workmanship of the wheels was like the workmanship of a chariot wheel; their axle pins, their rims, their spokes, and their hubs were all of cast bronze. 34 And there were four supports at the four corners of each cart; its supports were part of the cart itself. 35 On the top of the cart, at the height of half a cubit, it was perfectly round. And on the top of the cart, its flanges and its panels were of the same casting. 36 On the plates of its flanges and on its panels he engraved cherubim, lions, and palm trees, wherever there was a clear space on each, with wreaths all around. 37 Thus he made the ten carts. All of them were of the same mould, one measure, and one shape.

38 Then he made ten lavers of bronze; each laver contained forty baths, and each laver was four cubits. On each of the ten carts was

a laver. 39 And he put five carts on the right side of the house, and five on the left side of the house. He set the Sea on the right side of the house, toward the southeast.

40 Hurammade the lavers and the shovels and the bowls. So Huram finished doing all the work that he was to do for King Solomon for the house of the Lord: 41 the two pillars, the two bowl shaped capitals that were on top of the two pillars; the two networks covering the two bowl-shaped capitals which were on top of the pillars; 42 four hundred pomegranates for the two networks (two rows of pomegranates for each network, to cover the two bowl shaped capitals that were on top of the pillars); 43 the ten carts, and ten lavers on the carts; 44 one Sea, and twelve oxen under the Sea; 45 the pots, the shovels, and the bowls.

All these articles which Huram made for King Solomon for the house of the Lord were of burnished bronze. 46 In the plain of Jordan the king had them cast in clay molds, between Succoth and Zaretan. 47 And Solomon did not weigh all the articles, because there were so many; the weight of the bronze was not determined.

48 Thus Solomon had all the furnishings made for the house of the Lord: the altar of gold, and the table of gold on which was the showbread; 49 the lampstands of pure gold, five on the right side and five on the left in front of the inner sanctuary, with the flowers and the lamps and the wick-trimmers of gold; 50 the basins, the trimmers, the bowls, the ladles, and the censers of pure gold; and the hinges of gold, both for the doors of the inner room (the Most Holy Place) and for the doors of the main hall of the temple.

51 So all the work that King Solomon had done for the house of the Lord was finished; and Solomon brought in the things which his father David had dedicated: the silver and the gold and the furnishings. He put them in the treasuries of the house of the Lord. (1 kings 7:1-51)

"Behold, I have created the blacksmith who blows the coals in the fire, who brings forth an instrument for his work; and I have created the spoiler to destroy. No weapon formed against you shall prosper, and every tongue which rises against you in judgment you shall condemn.

This is the heritage of the servants of the Lord, and their righteousness is from me," says the Lord. (Isaiah 54:16-17)

It may not be so interesting when looking at and reading the above words but now I want to go a little deeper that you are saying to the maker of spears by putting iron in the furnace which is a very difficult job, but God has given strength to beat the iron. Outside of Nepal, the neighbouring country, the centre of the world, the small country, was attacked from all sides. The weapons made by this iron community defeated all the enemies.

In the context of Nepal, our Rai, Limbu, Gurung, Tamang community along with this Silpkar, Charmkar, Siojikar also lived together.

Children of Adam tailor sew clothes for the Mongolian community. God himself made leather jackets. Can we say that leather workers are sons and daughters of God or not?

My reference is to make pottery for the Mongolian community focused on blacksmithing, to make various tools for the farmers, to make jewellery. Our Mongolian sisters love a lot of jewellery. There were twenty-five, twenty-six kingdoms in Nepal, and this blacksmith community took the responsibility of making crowns and thrones for all the kings of those kingdoms, various weapons for killing, wild animals as well as weapons to fight and protect against enemies.

Priests carrying the ark resemble the musician tailor community in Nepal.

Panchebaja (a set of five traditional Nepali musical instruments played by the tailor community)

Priests used to blow the horn of a lamb.

Now they play Narsinga (Trumpet) in the context of Nepal.

Artisans used to inscribe the Bible on metal plates, and hide them underground, which preserved the Bible for modern humanity. Photo of a metal Bible

Tanners are mentioned in many places in the Bible. The same tanners are called Sarki in Nepali, and are designated as untouchables. Photo of a Parchment

Crown Cannon

Behold, I have created the smith that bloweth the coals in the fire, and that bringeth forth an instrument for his work; and I have created the waster to destroy. (Isaiah 54:16) In Indian context, this is about blacksmiths who are called Vishwakarma, which means those who can control the world by their actions.

In the context of Nepal, the blacksmiths who make crowns and create all the engineering equipment are called untouchable. Photos of a Turkish tailor and a Turkish leather drum

उत्पीडित दलित समुदायका घरहरू
विद्यमान छुवाछुत प्रथा तथा जातीय उत्पीडनको चरम शोषण दमनका कारण उत्पीडित दलित समुदायले आफ्नो धर्म संस्कृति, रीति-रिवाज एवं वंशज दर गोत्र लाई राज्य र समाजले अवरजस्त नामेट पार्ने अस्तित्व विहिन बनाए पनि सबै उत्पीडित दलित समुदायको पुर्खौली इतिहासको निरन्तरतामा आधारित भिन्न वर्गोत्तम काती र वर्गर पाइन्छन् । तर वर्तीयय भौगोलिक स्थिती, देशका स्थल तथा सामयिक परिवेशमा प्रचलनमा आउने भाषाका तवर वा उच्चारणका कारण केही थरहरू बौद्धिएका र नया प्रचलनमा न्वाइएकाले ठगशिक्षमा आलेख हुन आएका थरहरूले स्पष्ट प्रमाणित गर्ने आवश्यक इतिहासको जानकारका लिधि भिन्न वर्गोत्तम प्रस्तुत गरिएको छ ।

SURNAMES OF OPPRESSED DALIT COMMUNITY

Due to the extreme exploitation and oppression of the existing system of untouchability and caste oppression, the oppressed Dalit community's own religion, culture, customs and descendants, castes and castes are found as follows, based on the continuity of the waiting history of the self-oppressed Dalit community, although the state and society forcefully abolished their own religion, culture, customs and descendants, and castes. However, some surnames have been repeated and brought into new circulation due to some geographical location, occupation form and social environment. So, it is considered necessary to clearly prove the surnames that have been written in detail. So, it is presented as follows for discussion.

THE SINGING COMMUNITY (UNTOUCHABLES) Adhikari, Kami, Kalakaushik, Kala, Poudel, Kalichan, Gasai, Jogi, Thakuri, Turki, Bahun, Budhathoki, Baikar, Bagyakar, Vaistha, Bista, Bogte, Bhushal, Bhushalparvate, Maheshwar, Vishwakarma, Vishnupada, Samundri, Shai, Surasaman, Setaparvate, Setichan, Kukchingarana, etc.

Badi Community: (Untouchables)

Khati, Rasailithapa, Rasaily, Lekali, Chinal, Baral, Thakur, Rana, Kumal, Khadka, Jogi, Bote, Upadhyay, Rizal, Singh, Shrestha, Paudel, Adhikari, Kami, Damai, Badshah, Khan, Dhital, Niraula

SOME COMMUNITIES IN MADESH

(TERAI) (UNTOUCHABLES)

Chamar, Ram, Mahara, Mochi, Harijan, Doom, Dom, Sada, Madhouyasada, Jhagad, Ugau, Uram, Dusadh, Paswan, Jhagar, Kuchuva, Kharava, Bakla, Bujira, Bekh, Lakheda, Khachbe, Mandal, etc.

Details of all these communities are printed in government books with official seal and government seal.

Indigenous Gurungs also have many surnames. And some complain like this that Brahmins have made us Gurung and our caste has become

Gurung. More than ten other surnames are also found within the Gurung community. For example, Ghonde, Ghale, Lamichhane and so on. The government has given permission to modify any surname as you like. The reason must be shown, please wait. Balabhadra Kunwar revised Jang Bahadur Rana. Marichman Singh later added Shrestha. It cannot be changed but it can be amended.

VISHWAKARMA, SILPKAR COMMUNITY (UNTOUCHABLES)

Agri, Acharya, Afaldhoti, Od, Or, Kadara, Kallohar, Kalikote, Kaliraj, Shah, Kumarki, Kaini, Koli, Kairala, Khadthoki, Khapangi, Khati, Gajmer, Gajurel, Gadal, Gadaili, Gahatraj, Gahate, Giri, Gotame, Gava, Ghatani, Ghamal, Gharti, Ghimire, Ghamchatal, Ghatan, Chandara, Chuthara, Chalam, Chanara, Chistal, Jadkama, Tamata, Tamrakar, Thagunna, Thattra, Dhanuk, Nagarkoti, Niraula, Nepal, Panthi, Pallam, Parajuli, Pahri, Padhyavati, Parki, Pagri, Pokhrel, Partel, Barali, Baraili, Baral, Buchevale, Baskota, Bipali, Bhatt, Bhattarai, Bhusal, Bhul, Mahilpar, Mahar, Mar, Mizhar, Rasaily, Rahpal, Rajilehar, Ramdas, Ramudam, Rizal, Luhagun, Shankar, Shahshankar, Shahu, Sharela, Sob, Sadashankar, Sapkota,

Sani, Sundhuwa, Sunchyuri, Sigaure, Sijapati, Sipali, Sripali, Suni, Setipar, Setimahar, Setisural, Sonam, Swanarkar, Hemchayuri, etc.

The reason these communities are worshiped as Vishwakarma in India is the title of God given by the people of India who have acquired the ability to destroy the world (Isaiah 54:16). That is why they worship them instead of angering them.

The world is this earth and Karma is what they can do. They can disturb the state of the world. They make guns, gun-powder, bombs, assault weapons, as well as gold and silver items needed for auspicious work.

SARKI (TANNERS) COMMUNITY (UNTOUCHABLES)

Achhami, Achami, Uparkoti, Upreti, Kamar, Kisan, Koirala, Khatiwada, Giri, Gair, Gairipal, Gache, Ghimire, Chan, Chand, Charmkar, Sike, Gautama, Gotame, Chudal, Chuhan, Thagunn, Chmarki, Thakursya, Thadrai, Dalai, Dale, Tolangi, Thak, Thaplia, Thapa, Daulakoti, Dhaulakoti, Dabe, Dahal, Dulaal, Dhamel, Dhamala, Nadhali, Paheli, Payi, Purkoti, Pulami, Paudel, Bassel, Basyal, Bamrel, Byalkoti, Bastakota, Bisunkhe, Bogti, Bhagyal, Bheyal, Bhool, Bhurtel, Vipal, Maurati, Magrati, Magrati, Majakoti, Majavoti, Malvul, Malwok, Mudel, Ramtel, Raut, Rawat, Roila, Roka, Lamzel, Lamsal, Shahi, Shrimali, Siroyali, Siroute, Surkhet, Sanyal, Sejwal, Hamal, Hitang Hitagan, SK, etc.

Even these communities are forbidden to touch the corpse. Conch shells are not played during their festivals. In Jewish tradition, instruments were not played nor conch played during festivals.

"They shall not defile themselves by coming near a dead person. Only for father or mother, for son or daughter, for brother or unmarried sister may they defile themselves." (Ezekiel 44:25)

Today, we have God's word in our hands because they wrote the word of God on the skin and kept it carefully. Hating these communities as Dalits is stressing God. Simon and Paul were Jewish tanners.

"Send therefore to Joppa and call Simon here, whose surname is Peter. He is lodging in the house of Simon, a tanner, by the sea." (Acts 10:32)

SAGUNE (GOOD-OMEN OR PRIESTLY) COMMUNITY

Sagune community is understood as a community that worships by playing instruments in auspicious activities. According to the Bible, the Sagune community belongs to the tribe of Levi.

Sagune Community or auspicious Community (Untouchables)

Adhikari, Assay, Auji, Kandel, Katuwal, Karkidholi, Khulal, Mudula, Lama, Sutar, Kalakhati, Koirala, Khatiwada, Khali, Gautam, Gotame, Ghatani, Ghale, Chahar, Chuhan, Chinal, Jairu, Thagunna, Thatal, Daude, Dhayaki, Tiwari, Trikhatri, Thapa, Darnal, Damai, Pariyar, Parel, Das, Dewas, Nagwan, Nagrchi, Negi, Nepali, Nepal, Nauwag, Achhame, Chudal, Paribag, Pant, Pahari, Panchkoti, Panchakoti, Pokharel, Bardev, Bahak, Bagchan, Bagdas, Budhathoki, Baiju, Bhandari, Bhattarai, Intrakoti, Bhusal, Magar, Mahate, Mahara, Male, Rajbar, Ranpal, Ranpaheli, Ranpaili, Ratna, Ratnapariyar, Rana, Rai, Raigai, Raaka, Chaizhyai, Lapre, Lamaghate, Luitel, Sinal, Silal, Siba, Siwa, Kukhure, Gatame, Bhede, Siladhar, Seva, Syawa, Sunam, Sundas, Suname, Sunal, Sunburi, Sasmundra, Samundshahi, Suja, Hidammang, Hudke, Aptayara, Thul, Verikar, Betuwa, Tiral, Retan, Bitalu, Nagarkoti, Marte, Yagne, Karnal, Kamero, Badaro, Tamke, Tapyaanko, Magle, Subhash, Sagune, Durge, Siy, Vanadar, Bhauke, Dhake, Dimdime, etc. surnames are found. The communities with these surnames are special

1. Adam made clothes and these communities have received the gift of making clothes.

   "Then the eyes of both of them were opened, and they knew that they were naked; and they sewed fig leaves together and made themselves coverings." (Genesis 3:7)

2. According to the book of Exodus they were skilled in making the clothes of the temple and the priests and the people who served in the temple. (Exodus 31:1-11; Leviticus 7:1-6)

In earlier history of Nepal, during the Dashain festival when animal sacrifice was made, the tail had to be given for this community. Now the community is also called tail-eating community. In addition, they are said to be holy communities who play trumpets in any auspicious event, temple dedication ceremonies, inaugurations, vigils in the army, play fiddles, as well as being the first to reach the summit of the hill and blowing the *karnal* trumpet (horn) to invite, blowing the trumpet as messengers.

ANOTHER BIBLICAL BASIS

After any crop was harvested and fruits were borne, this community had to be allocated a portion. Either they would come to pick it up themselves, or they had to be delivered it. The first part of the harvest was mandatory.

25 "They shall not defile themselves by coming near a dead person. Only for father or mother, for son or daughter, for brother or unmarried sister may they defile themselves. 26 After he is cleansed, they shall count seven days for him. 27 And on the day that he goes to the sanctuary to minister in the sanctuary, he must offer his sin offering in the inner court," says the Lord God. 28 "It shall be, in regard to their inheritance, that I am their inheritance. You shall give them no possession in Israel, for I am their possession. 29 They shall eat the grain offering, the sin offering, and the trespass offering; every dedicated thing in Israel shall be theirs. 30 The best of all first fruits of any kind, and every sacrifice of any kind from all your sacrifices, shall be the priest's; also you shall give to the priest the first of your ground meal, to cause a blessing to rest on your house. 31The priests shall not eat anything, bird or beast, that died naturally or was torn by wild beasts. (Ezekiel 44:25-31)

In the Bible, these communities were forbidden to touch the dead body or even go to the funeral process, now it is also forbidden in Nepal.

Outside of the Christian society, the untouchability in the four groups or communities is everywhere. But this is a tragedy that because of the greater racial conflict within our Christian society I have tried to prove it from the word of God. I have already given evidence about whose children we are, by saying that we are all the children of Adam tailor and Eve Damini. Because cloth makers in Nepal have been called Dalit for years as a small caste.

Another leather worker has also been given the Dalit name of Sarki. But in fact, God Himself made leather jackets for Adam and Eve and sewed them. What can we say about it?

When Nepali Christians give an example, they often say that they are like the Samaritans. Especially the pastors of the Brahmin class understand the Samaritans as Dalits, untouchables, and low class. Now, my Brahmin class pastors, my Mongolian class pastors, my untouchable class pastors please read this verse – "Then the king of Assyria brought people from Babylon, Cuthah, Ava, Hamath, and from Sepharvaim, and placed them in the cities of Samaria instead of the children of Israel; and they took possession of Samaria and dwelt in its cities." (2 Kings 17:24)

They were settled in the cities of Samaria instead of the Israel. They brought them (that is, the entire northern kingdom) to settle in the cities of Assyria in order to destroy even a little bit of nationalism that was left in them. The relationship between the Israelites who were taken to Assyria and the Assyrians was not established, but the marriage relationship between the Israelites who were there was established with the foreigners who were brought to Israel. And their mixed offspring born to those foreigners were called "Samaritans." As a result, foreign religions and cultural traditions became mixed with Hebrew practices and beliefs. By the time of the New Testament, however, many Samaritans had abandoned their gentile practices and believed entirely in the faith based on the first five books of the Pentateuch. 29 However every nation continued to make gods of its own, and put them in the shrines on the high places which the Samaritans had made, every nation in the cities where they dwelt. 30 The men of Babylon made Succoth Benoth, the men of Cuth made Nergal, the men of Hamath made Ashima, 31 and the Avites made Nibhaz and Tartak; and the Sepharvites burned their children in fire to Adrammelech and Anammelech, the gods of Sepharvaim. (2 Kings 17:29-31)

The seven Dalit communities mentioned above neither built temples nor did they intermarry, nor do they sacrifice their own sons and daughters by making foreign national gods. For Christians to compare the people of our Dalit community with the Samaritans and to mark them as Samaritans and to name them as idolaters becomes a very big crime.

Now, we will see the background of who the untouchables are. After bringing them out of Egypt, we will read the Ten Commandments given by God.

And God spoke all these words, saying: 2 "I am the Lord your God, who brought you out of the land of Egypt, out of the house of bondage." 3 "You shall have no other gods before Me." 4 "You shall not make for yourself a carved image—any likeness of anything that is in heaven above, or that is in the earth beneath, or that is in the water under the earth; 5 you shall not bow down to them nor serve them. For I, the Lord your God, am a jealous God." (Exodus 20:1-5a)

I, the author myself, would like to thank my Brahmin community from the bottom of my heart. Of course, mistakes were made by you in the past days. But it is not necessary to accept all the allegations. You forbade the untouchables to worship bronze, metal, clay, and wood created by themselves in a respectable language. This is a very good job.

All these things should be understood by the untouchables and the facts should be found out. On the contrary, by threatening and insulting, forced injustice happened. We have been accused of violating human rights.

It is not your fault that you could not understand the soft civilized language from you. You Brahmin scholars have not done any injustice to them. You said untouchable, but they didn't understand. You nature worshipers, do not touch us. Do not come to our temple and do not come to our house.

After they did not understand the meaning of the word untouchable, the word Dalit was used. It sounds a bit harsh but another Sanskrit word for Dalit is Harijan. Hari means creator in Sanskrit. Jan (People) are the sons and daughters of the creator and we have not worshiped artifacts for years. You are saying, "Don't worship now." Even Mahatma Gandhi said that Harijans were sons and daughters of God. He was speaking a profound truth, even if he may not have fully understood the implication of his own statement!

But I have a request to my Brahmin Pundits also and please think and look carefully. Do not insist that only the sons and daughters of untouchable Harijan, the children of God, should not worship the artifacts of the artisans or sculptors. Stop worshiping the art of sculptors yourself. Search for the creator who created man. Your activities will neither forgive you from your sin nor bring you to heaven. You don't have to make sacrifices every year on Dashain and ask for forgiveness of your sins. Lord Jesus has been sacrificed on the cross bearing the sins of the whole world. He was sacrificed, killed, buried, and ascended to heaven. The living Jesus hears your prayers.

Over the years, Talasi and Khelasi as well as historians have prepared various materials in an attempt to understand it in different ways and have gone to different places and researched geography as well as different languages and communities. This process continues. An attempt was also made to give a reasonable answer. People are trying to stop the conflict between people through different means with journalists in assembly meetings.

I am also one of them. From the age of four, I tried to seek answers to the questions like: Why was I born? Why should I live? Where will I go after death? These kinds of thoughts have been holding this Brahmin. Sun, moon, stars, wind, we are responsible in different ways. But we are looking for our roots. While searching for the roots, why did the research on friendship continue? And about untouchability, who should not touch whom? Even we should drink water from them? Untouchable? 16 And what agreement has the temple of God with idols? For you are the temple of the living God. As God has said, "I will dwell in them and walk among them. I will be their God, and they shall be my people." 17 Therefore "Come out from among them and be separate," says the Lord. Do not touch what is unclean, and I will receive you." 18 "I will be a Father to you, and you shall be my sons and daughters," says the LORD Almighty. (2 Corinthians 6:16-18)

From this Bible verse we can easily understand that there are idol worshipers in our country, who want to look like Aryans as Jews. The

Jews were commanded not to worship idols in the Ten Commandments. Most of the untouchables in Nepal do not even worship idols and the idol worshipers have also told you not to touch us and the untouchables have been told not to touch the idol worshippers.

In Exodus 3:7, God says to the Dalits in Nepal, "I have surely seen the oppression and I have heard their cry."

Exodus 5:1 says, "Let my people go."

In Exodus 8:1, God says, "Let My people go that they may serve me."

At that time, the Jews were treated as untouchables by the Egyptians. Now our idolatrous Brahmins did not treat all Dalits as harshly as the Pharaoh did.

Another nickname of Dalits in India which was given by Mahatma Gandhi. They are not Dalits, they are Harijans.

Hari in Sanskrit means creator or father

- Created to be worshipped

- Sons and daughters of the Creator

- King Jesus' people. In the book of Corinthians in the New Testament, the readers are forbidden to touch unclean things and someone's dead body, and Dalits are not allowed to touch dead bodies. I request my untouchable Harijans not to eat or drink touched by idol worshippers.

I started by mentioning the disease at the beginning. Where do we come from? Who are we? Different communities trampled each other, clashed, uttered various abusive words and endured hurtful words until they reached here. We do not need to be confused. We all are the children of Adam.

God

Adam

Noah

I have given you about the history of the Aryans from my dear brother, who deserves my utmost respect.

LOWLY DALIT

1 The vision of Obadiah. Thus says the Lord God concerning Edom (We have heard a report from the Lord, and a messenger has been sent among the nations, saying, "Arise, and let us rise up against her for battle") 2 "Behold, I will make you small among the nations; you shall be greatly despised. 3 The pride of your heart has deceived you, you who dwell in the clefts of the rock, whose habitation is high; you who say in your heart, 'Who will bring me down to the ground?'4 Though you ascend as high as the eagle, and though you set your nest among the stars, from there I will bring you down," says the Lord. 5 "If thieves had come to you, If robbers by night—Oh, how you will be cut off— Would they not have stolen till they had enough? If grape-gatherers had come to you, would they not have left some gleanings? 6 "Oh, how Esau shall be searched out! How his hidden treasures shall be sought after!7 All the men in your confederacy shall force you to the border; the men at peace with you shall deceive you and prevail against you. Those who eat your bread shall lay a trap for you. No one is aware of it. 8 "Will I not in that day," says the Lord, "Even destroy the wise men from Edom, and understanding from the mountains of Esau? 9 Then your mighty men, O Teman, shall be dismayed, to the end that everyone from the mountains of Esau may be cut off by slaughter. 10 "For violence against your brother Jacob, shame shall cover you, and you shall be cut off forever. 11 In the day that you stood on the other side—In the day that strangers carried captive his forces, when foreigners entered his gates and cast lots for Jerusalem—Even you were as one of them. 12 "But you should not have gazed on the day of your brother in the day of his captivity; nor should you have rejoiced over the children of Judah in the day of their destruction; nor should you have spoken proudly in the day of distress. 13 You should not have entered the gate of my people in the day of their calamity. Indeed, you should not have gazed

on their affliction in the day of their calamity, nor laid hands on their substance in the day of their calamity. 14 You should not have stood at the crossroads to cut off those among them who escaped; nor should you have delivered up those among them who remained in the day of distress. 15 "For the day of the Lord upon all the nations is near; as you have done, it shall be done to you; your reprisal shall return upon your own head. 16 For as you drank on My holy mountain, so shall all the nations drink continually; yes, they shall drink, and swallow, and they shall be as though they had never been. 17 "But on Mount Zion there shall be deliverance, and there shall be holiness; the house of Jacob shall possess their possessions. 18 The house of Jacob shall be a fire, and the house of Joseph a flame; but the house of Esau shall be stubble; they shall kindle them and devour them, and no survivor shall remain of the house of Esau," For the Lord has spoken. (Obadiah 1:1-18)

In Nepali society, we were taught that Brahma created five types of people. When the division of caste system is explained, it is said that Shudra is made from legs. That's why the idea has been engraved in our brain since ancient time. Its effect has been like the root of a very deep disease and the interpretation of *Chudra* in Nepali is understood as petty, lowly indecent behaviour. In fact, such low and indecent behaviour seems to be the person who has the mindset that he is a person of high class and caste. The teaching that Brahma created five types of people is only imaginary. It has no basis at all.

"Behold, I will make you small among the nations; you shall be greatly despised. The pride of your heart has deceived you, you who dwell in the clefts of the rock, whose habitation is high; you who say in your heart, 'Who will bring me down to the ground?' Though you ascend as high as the eagle, and though you set your nest among the stars, from there I will bring you down," says the Lord.

God has said about Edom that these Edomites were so proud and they would say that no one knew better than them. Those who consider themselves to be equal to God will persecute those who worship the true God and stop worshiping other idols.

Then your mighty men, O Teman, shall be dismayed, to the end that everyone from the mountains of Esau may be cut off by slaughter. "For violence against your brother Jacob, shame shall cover you, and you shall be cut off forever."

TRADITION: HOW DASHAIN FESTIVAL STARTED

We who live in Asia often like to listen to oral history. Our forefathers also told us different kinds of stories. How the tradition starts, Pundit Resham Raj Paudel used to tell two examples.

There was a family in one of the villages of Nepal who tied up a cat for *sraddha* – a ceremony related to the veneration of the dead ancestors. That family also had a cat during sraddha, because milk and curd is often needed in the ceremony so the cat should not touch the materials used in that ceremony. Most of the time, during the dedication, the cat was tied to a corner. There were three generations in that family, for example, the grandson used to watch grandfather's ceremony performed by his father for years. Years passed, the father passed away and the grandson grew up. Now, it was the grandson's turn to do the ceremony for his father, and in the grandson's turn, there was no cat. So, the cat was taken from the neighbour's house or rented for a few hours. This custom may have led to the business of renting out cats in that village and some may have become rich. Whatever it is, what we need to know is how it started, but we often don't ask.

We have been giving recognition to various customs. Likewise, it is time for us to inquire. Maybe the sradha stopped because he didn't get a cat? Perhaps, no one told you that veneration can be done even without tying a cat? Perhaps, even the Pundit Ji would not tell you? Maybe, the Pundit didn't know about that? It is time to question how the custom started rather than the custom itself. This is an example in Nepal. In a family outside of Nepal, when cooking fish, it was always cooked by discarding the head and half of the belly of the fish. Almost everywhere in that region, the old mother used to cook food for the family at home. Then, the old mother passed away. It was mother's turn, mother also used to throw away half of the fish while cooking. As this happened, many generations passed in that family, maybe because of that old mother's custom, her sons and grandsons filled the village and the custom stayed there. Perhaps, the members of that family have reached the corner of the world through education, trade, business as well as marriage. Maybe that custom has reached everywhere and it has become a tradition or culture. But suddenly, a little girl was born in the same tradition. One day, when her mother brought fish and threw away half of it to cook, the little girl asked, "Mother, why is it that only half of the fish is cooked in our family? Why is the whole fish not cooked?" Maybe, the mother would have answered, "My little girl, being such a child, you would ask such a big question. This is our culture. How it came and why it came is not the matter." Maybe, the mother would have scolded her. She may have been beaten or punished by her mother or a family member because she was asking. But no matter what happened, the girl did not stay silent. It was her desire or curiosity to know. How did the custom of cooking this fish by cutting it in half come about? She starts researching about where it came from. After many years of research and effort, she found out that many years ago, in that family, which had introduced this practice, there was only a small cooking pan. Because of that pan this practice (culture) came about. The grandmother was the one who introduced this culture in the family. No one dared to ask, but it was discovered through the efforts of the little girl. Because the fish was big and the pan was small, half of the fish was thrown away. Nowadays, you can find big pan or small pan and fish can be cooked in half or full or it can be cooked three or four times. Traditions and customs can be discovered with questions and curiosity like that of a little girl.

We give this answer many times. Our priests and wise sages who have studied the Vedas and scriptures would say, "Do you think you know better? Shame on you for asking these kinds of questions."

Now let's talk about how Dussehra started. We can understand it in four ways: one is a sacrifice of repentance, two is the story of Esther, three is the arrival of a king of the Shah dynasty in Nepal, and four is Arya's rule over the Indians or Mongolians in India.

HARIJAN OR GOD'S PEOPLE

Afterward Moses and Aaron went in and told Pharaoh, "Thus says the Lord God of Israel: 'Let My people go, that they may hold a feast to me in the wilderness.'" And Pharaoh said, "Who is the Lord, that I should obey His voice to let Israel go? I do not know the Lord, nor will I let Israel go." (Exodus 5:1-2)

Afterward, Moses and Aaron went in and told Pharaoh, "Thus says the Lord God of Israel: 'Let My people go, that they may hold a feast to me in the wilderness.'" We will go back a little bit in history to see why God said this.

THE OPPRESSION OF THE ISRAELITES IN EGYPT

Now these are the names of the children of Israel who came to Egypt; each man and his household came with Jacob: Reuben, Simeon, Levi, and Judah; Issachar, Zebulun, and Benjamin; Dan, Naphtali, Gad, and Asher. All those who were descendants of Jacob were seventy persons (for Joseph was in Egypt already). And Joseph died, all his brothers, and all that generation. But the children of Israel were fruitful and increased abundantly, multiplied and grew exceedingly mighty; and the land was filled with them.

Now there arose a new king over Egypt, who did not know Joseph. And he said to his people, "Look, the people of the children of Israel are more and mightier than we; come, let us deal shrewdly with them, lest they multiply, and it happen, in the event of war, that they also join our enemies and fight against us, and so go up out of the land."

Therefore, they set taskmasters over them to afflict them with their burdens. And they built for Pharaoh supply cities, Pithom and Raamses. But the more they afflicted them, the more they multiplied and grew.

THE TAILOR COMMUNITY

Adhikari, Assay, Auji, Kadel, Katuwal, Karkidauli, Khulal, Mudula, Lama, Sutar, Kalakhati, Koirala, Khatiwada, Khati, Guide, Gotam, Gotame, Ghatani, Ghale, Chahar, Chuhan, Chinal, Jairu, Thagunna,Thatal, Daude, Dhyak, Tiwari, Trikhatri, Thapa, Darnal, Damai, Pariyar, Parel, Das, Debus, Nagwan, Nagarchi, Negi, Nepali, Nepal, Nauwag, Achhome, Chudal, Paribag, Pant, Pahari, Panchkoti, Panchakoti, Pokharel, Bardeb, Bahak, Bagchan, Bagdas, Budhathoki, Baiju, Bhandari, Bhattarai, Intrakoti, Bhusal, Magar, Mahte, Mahara, Male, Rajwar, Khapal, Ranpaheli, Ranpaili, Ratna, Ratne, Ratnapariyar, Rana, Rai, Raigai, Raaka, Chaizhyai, Lapre, Lamaghate, Luitel, Shinal, Shilal, Shiba, Siva, Kukhure, Gotame, Bhede, Shilaghar, Seba, Syawa, Sunam, Sundas, Suname, Sunal, Sunchyuri, Sasmundra, Samundrashai, Suja, Hingmang, Hudke, Aptyara, Dhakel, Bherikar, Betuwa, Tiral, Thatal, Retan, Vitalu, Nagarkoti, Marte, Yagne, Karnal, Kamero, Bataro, Tamke, Taryanko, Magle, Subhash, Sagune, Durge, Siy, Banadar, Bhauke, Dhake, Divdive, etc. There are 60 types of surnames.

Adam, the first man, made the first clothes. Different terms are used to call this community: Siojikar in Nepali, tailor in English, Talmud in Hebrew, and darzi in Hindi and Urdu. "So, when the woman saw that the tree was good for food, that it was pleasant to the eyes, and a tree desirable to make one wise, she took of its fruit and ate. She also gave to her husband with her, and he ate. Then the eyes of both of them were opened, and they knew that they were naked; and they sewed fig leaves together and made themselves coverings." (Genesis 3:6-7)

The gods of India and Nepal are wearing clothes, but who made the clothes? Even Mahatma Gandhi made his own clothes. Do you call him untouchable?

It is written in the Bible that God made men and women, but God made five types of men in India and Nepal. Who made women? Or from which country were the women brought?

It is written in the Bible, "These were the families of the sons of Noah, according to their generations, in their nations; and from these, the nations were divided on the earth after the flood." (Genesis 10:32)

Brahma made man in India. This story and the story of Ramayana is limited to Sri Lanka, India, and Nepal. Who made man in other countries?

HARIJAN

Harijan (Hindusthani: Devanagari Nastalik; Translation: Children of God) They were called sons and daughters of God during Mahatma Gandhi's time.

Gandhi used to say, "It is a common mistake to use the word untouchable because if they are Harijans, Harijans are God's children, even in Gujarat, Dalits are called Harijans or God's people."

In the Bible, Harijan means sons and daughters of God and is found in many places.

Afterward, Moses and Aaron went in and told Pharaoh, "Thus says the Lord God of Israel: 'Let My people go, that they may hold a feast to me in the wilderness.'" (Exodus 5:1)

And you shall say to him, 'The Lord God of the Hebrews has sent me to you, saying, "Let My people go, that they may serve me in the wilderness"; but indeed, until now you would not hear! (Exodus 7:16)

Then the Lord said to Moses, "Go to Pharaoh and tell him, 'Thus says the Lord God of the Hebrews: "Let My people go, that they may serve Me." (Exodus 9:1)

So Moses and Aaron came in to Pharaoh and said to him, "Thus says the Lord God of the Hebrews: 'How long will you refuse to humble yourself before Me? Let My people go, that they may serve Me.'" (Exodus 10:3)

"You are the children of the Lord your God; you shall not cut yourselves nor shave the front of your head for the dead. (Deuteronomy 14:1)

My people are destroyed for lack of knowledge. Because you have rejected knowledge, I also will reject you from being priest for Me; because you have forgotten the law of your God, I also will forget your children. (Hosea 4:6)

They shall not defile themselves anymore with their idols, nor with their detestable things, nor with any of their transgressions; but I will deliver them from all their dwelling places in which they have sinned, and will cleanse them. Then, they shall be My people, and I will be their God. (Ezekiel 37:23)

79 Do not be unequally yoked together with unbelievers. For what fellowship has righteousness with lawlessness? And what communion has light with darkness? (2 Corinthians 6:14)

And because you are sons, God has sent forth the Spirit of His Son into your hearts, crying out, "Abba, Father!" (Galatians 4:6)

WHERE DID THE CHUDRAS (LOWLY PEOPLE) COME FROM?

Dr Bal Krishna says in Caste System in Nepal (p.107), "Another evidence for the existence of caste in Nepal was that many inscriptions issued by *Licchavi* rulers address the villagers and inhabitants as those led by Brahmans. This inscriptive evidence certainly presupposes a society with a caste structure. We do not know exactly the orthodoxy of the unorthodoxy of the people. Though the caste system was introduced in the society it was not rigid because a give and take policy was very much emphasized. Also, the Licchavis were not considered Pure Hindus by the Hindus of the plain. We cannot accept such impure Licchavis introducing the rigid caste structure at the beginning state. Describing the position of different caste groups D.R. Regmi says, "The Brahmans are called the members of highest caste. They administered to ritual which had then become part of social life. In that capacity, they commanded respect and influence among their followers. But we know very little about their laity. The Kshatriyas, of course, were there; so also the Vaishyas. But we know little of the Shudra and lower caste."

CONCEPT OF DALIT NON-GOVERNMENTAL ORGANIZATION FEDERATION

The concept of varna (caste-complexion) system is an ancient concept of Hinduism. When the system of untouchability was introduced in the Indian system, it did not keep only the pure in the untouchable class, but those who followed hard and disgusting professions having blood relation with that class, those who were caste-reduced as punishment by the state and the poor and helpless of the society involved in criminal activities started to be kept in this untouchable class. They were seen as a supposedly 'untouchable' non-water caste. In the course of time, the custom of calling Dalit caste to the various castes which are said to be untouchable emerged.

Chapter 4

History of the Shah Dynasty

BEGINNING OF THE SHAH DYNASTY

It is well known that Christians are being persecuted even in countries with the symbol of a snake (a dangerous snake) on the flag. God created all things and living animals. Among the creatures that God created, the snake was cunning and it deceived God's sons and daughters, Eve and Adam, to break the commandment and sin began in the world. Later, God spoke of the birth of Jesus through the Virgin Mary to conquer Satan, and Jesus was born to crush the head of Satan the serpent. He was sacrificed on the cross, buried in the tomb, and rose from the dead. The tomb was emptied and he went to heaven victoriously. From the beginning, the desire of the serpent – the desire of the devil – is to lead away the sons and daughters of God, to surprise, to separate from the presence of God, to destroy, and to spoil. The serpent is called the father of lies in the Bible. In the same way, in the beginning, a man named Joseph was sold into Egypt. They became servants, children were born and they began to increase in number, but the king of Egypt persecuted those children of Joseph in a cruel way. God brought his people out of Egypt and into the Promised Land through the hands of Moses. This struggle was not easy, but God's powerful hand pulled them out.

We will pay attention to the pharaoh, the king of Egypt. A host of serpents are seen on the crown and royal throne of the pharaoh. A Cobra is seen in the front part of the crown and cobras are seen on the throne of the throne covering the head from above and behind. Was it the Egyptians or the people who were hostile to God the Creator? The Pharaoh did not let God's people go easily. When studying the crown and the throne of the kings in the world, there is also a cobra on the crown of the king of Egypt and the cobras are also protecting the king of Nepal from behind.

It was there that Pharaoh asked Moses, "I do not know who God is."

It is understood that the deep meaning of this is that I am God myself. Similarly, the Shah Dynasty king of Nepal in the past was also considered as a symbol of Lord Vishnu and our history shows that the then king also accepted that. How did the heads of the snakes come to the throne of the Shah Dynasty king of Nepal? Probably not everyone knows about this mysterious history or hidden truth, about the migration of Pharaoh's children from Egypt to Iraq, Iran, and other Arab countries. Our Shah's ancestors are found in Iran and Arabia. There was also a dynasty of kings in Iran. Although the descendants of those kings lived in India and had Egyptian blood, they became Hindu, entered Nepal and defeated the Mongolian kingdoms, the descendants of Benei Manasseh, and started Vijayadashami. After attacking the Mongolian aboriginals and directly defeating the Nepali aboriginal people, religious laws were imposed starting from Vijayadashami. It is important for us to understand the unknown power of the snake more than the Shah dynasty. We studied a few glimpses before and will do so later that the descendants of Benei Manasseh were Jews.

A woman named Hagar, born in Egypt, was Abraham's servant. Abraham's seed Ishmael and the root of Islam are also confirmed to be from Egypt. Christians are persecuted in the Islamic countries. In the same way, Prithvi Narayan Shah exterminated the aboriginal people and deported some Christians and priests as we know from our history.

THE DRAGON IN THE BOOK OF REVELATION

And war broke out in heaven: Michael and his angels fought with the dragon; and the dragon and his angels fought. (Revelation 12:7)

Now, the beast which I saw was like a leopard, his feet were like the feet of a bear, and his mouth like the mouth of a lion. The dragon gave him his power, his throne, and great authority. (Revelation 13:2)

He laid hold of the dragon, that serpent of old, who is the Devil and Satan, and bound him for a thousand years. (Revelation 20:2)

And another sign appeared in heaven: behold, a great, fiery red dragon having seven heads and ten horns, and seven diadems on his heads. (Revelation 12:3)

There is a deep meaning behind the seven dragon symbols behind the thrones of our past Shah Dynasty kings. The Bible talks about snakes in many places. So, we don't need much more explanation. Shah Dynasty kings could not settle in any country. They had been persecuting Jews and Christians since the beginning.

Switzerland, a small country, is one of the richest and strongest countries in the world. There was a struggle before, but the people of the four communities who lived there have agreed to make a covenant with God and made the country blessed and stable. A cross has been placed on the flag of their country. The constitution there is also based on the words of the Bible. It is very deep and meaningful.

For example, there are other such countries in the world. As we see now, America is seen as a very powerful and rich country. The deep secret of this is that if the Israelites who believe in God had not been in America, the country would not be great. American Christians have understood this secret. We see that America loves and helps Israel through various means. The reason for this is because of the rich and knowledgeable people, who are no revealed in America. And the people who give advice in the parliament are the same Jews. Those who live in our country dream and plan to make it like the Christian country living in America, Israel and Europe and send their children to study and work there and dream of developing the country with the grants sent from the Christian country, but they chase and persecute Nepali Christians living in Nepal. Until the Christians are given the full rights, there can be no development in the country.

At the present time, until we Christians are placed in the first rank of citizens by the state and that behaviour is not done in the same way, democracy is and will continue to be just empty words.

Of course, when the Shah Dynasty kings attacked the Mongol kingdom, they were not victorious. How to consider it? Did not they have plenty of weapons or the strategy of the Shah Dynasty king by feeding or drinking alcohol to all these drunkards?

Of course, the Shah Dynasty king won. Our Lichchavi kings had to face defeat. Vedic scriptures about this war, gods and demons started as a great fantasy Vijayadashami. In reality, the demon is what our Licchhavi community was made of. As a deity, the Shah Dynasty occupied it and started Vijayadashami with a collective announcement.

My dear Mongolian brothers and sisters, walk with tika on their foreheads and celebrate happily on the day of Vijayadashami. The day of killing a grandfather should be mourned by dusting ashes, but they celebrate Vijayadashami of the attacking enemy by drinking alcohol. This does not mean that the blacksmith brothers made weak weapons, nor does it mean to blame them for making few weapons. But the next war was defeated by the British because of the *khukri* and guns made by our dear ones. Of course, even if brave Gorkhali succeeded in chasing the British, the blacksmith community who made tools and weapons and equipped them deserves no less thanks.

The crown, royal throne, as well as complete metal arms, temple accessories and accessories used by the kings of different states of Nepal were made by blacksmiths, Sarkis (tanners) and Damais (tailors). Let's discuss something about India. There is a custom of worshiping Vishwakarma Lord by making a figure in India. Why?

In Isaiah 54:16 and 17, the blacksmith who destroys the rebellion is exactly the same. Karma or work spoils whatever it does. So, the people thought, let us worship with the title of God. This community will not destroy our India and it was named Vishwakarma. In India, it is customary to respect a person who does something good as god. As I have mentioned above, I have been given the surname or caste of Kami because I worked hard with a big hummer. But Kami is also written as Devi while researching in Japanese language.

We have not only taken evidence from the Bible about the Kami community. Apart from the Bible, it is also proved by the customs of Nepal and the interpretation of Vishwakarma in India.

Kami in a Japanese word is for worship and is said to be the powerful force of the god of life, soul and body.

Please visit the above link. Everything is written in English and explained in a very interesting way.

Looking at the basis of profession or India's respect for Vishwakarma altogether, there is no hideous low-level calling or work or negative reasons and there is no place to blame these communities.

Even more noteworthy, the word of God was found in various places hidden in the ground under the soil, made into a metal book.

At that time, it was very difficult to transfer or write the words spoken by God on metal. Metal had to be found; stone coal had to be made. In order to complete all these tasks, the entire family as well as the whole community must have been involved.

At that time, to write one word on God's metal must have been very hard and our mind cannot imagine it. Here, the art, gift, and even better, skill given to this community by God is written as it is. To call and consider untouchable the society who made not only the temple but also brought God's word among us is insulting the Creator who made us human.

In Nepal, most of the skin-related communities are looked down upon as Sarkis and are considered low-level citizens in the society. This point of view seems to have a more profound effect on Christian society as well.

WHAT IS SARKI?

Untouchable. Why are you called untouchable? If they are said to be untouchable because they work with leather, what about the Sarkis who do not work with leather? We will do some deep study on this topic. Most of the low caste Nepalese do not hesitate to answer because of leather working.

Then, the eyes of both of them were opened, and they knew that they were naked; and they sewed fig leaves together and made themselves coverings. (Genesis 3:7)

Adam tailor and Eve tailor made clothes because people were naked after sinning. Then it is written, "Also for Adam and his wife the Lord God made tunics of skin, and clothed them." (Genesis 3:21)

God made leather clothes, jackets or long coats. We become the sons of God after accepting Christ completely. But is there no racial discrimination in the church?

Adam is the father of all of us. Adam tailor sewed the clothes. Now, what do we say to God who sews a leather jacket? God Sarki? Are we sons and daughters of God? Is God's name Sarki Bahadur?

Is there a custom to target Damai, Kami, Saraki as Samaritans by the pastors of our Brahmin community even now?

[4] And Moses spoke to all the congregation of the children of Israel, saying, "This is the thing which the Lord commanded, saying, [5] 'Take from among you an offering to the Lord. Whoever is of a willing heart, let him bring it as an offering to the Lord: gold, silver, and bronze; [6] blue, purple, and scarlet thread, fine linen, and goats' hair; [7] ram skins dyed red, badger skins, and acacia wood. (Exodus 35:4-7)

Ram skins dyed red, badger skins, and acacia wood are mentioned. Here also in the sacred place, people who work with leather are given skills.

Then Moses gathered all the congregation of the children of Israel together, and said to them, "These are the words which the Lord has commanded you to do: ² *Work shall be done for six days, but the seventh day shall be a holy day for you, a Sabbath of rest to the Lord. Whoever does any work on it shall be put to death.* ³ *You shall kindle no fire throughout your dwellings on the Sabbath day."*

⁴ *And Moses spoke to all the congregation of the children of Israel, saying, "This is the thing which the Lord commanded, saying:* ⁵ *'Take from among you an offering to the Lord. Whoever is of a willing heart, let him bring it as an offering to the Lord: gold, silver, and bronze;* ⁶ *blue, purple, and scarlet thread, fine linen, and goats' hair;* ⁷ *ram skins dyed red, badger skins, and acacia wood;* ⁸ *oil for the light, and spices for the anointing oil and for the sweet incense;* ⁹ *onyx stones, and stones to be set in the ephod and in the breastplate.*

¹⁰ *'All who are gifted artisans among you shall come and make all that the Lord has commanded:* ¹¹ *the tabernacle, its tent, its covering, its clasps, its boards, its bars, its pillars, and its sockets;* ¹² *the ark and its poles, with the mercy seat, and the veil of the covering;* ¹³ *the table and its poles, all its utensils, and the showbread;* ¹⁴ *also the lampstand for the light, its utensils, its lamps, and the oil for the light;* ¹⁵ *the incense altar, its poles, the anointing oil, the sweet incense, and the screen for the door at the entrance of the tabernacle;* ¹⁶ *the altar of burnt offering with its bronze grating, its poles, all its utensils, and the laver and its base;* ¹⁷ *the hangings of the court, its pillars, their sockets, and the screen for the gate of the court;* ¹⁸ *the pegs of the tabernacle, the pegs of the court, and their cords;* ¹⁹ *the garments of ministry, for ministering in the holy place—the holy garments for Aaron the priest and the garments of his sons, to minister as priests.'"*

²⁰*And all the congregation of the children of Israel departed from the presence of Moses.* ²¹ *Then everyone came whose hear was stirred, and everyone whose spirit was willing, and they brought the Lord's offering for the work of the tabernacle of meeting, for all its service, and for the holy garments.* ²² *They came, both men and women, as many as had a willing heart, and brought earrings and nose rings, rings and necklaces, all jewellery of gold, that is, every man who made an offering of gold to the Lord.* ²³*And every man, with whom was found blue, purple, and scarlet thread, fine*

linen, and goats' hair, red skins of rams, and badger skins, brought them. ²⁴ Everyone who offered an offering of silver or bronze brought the Lord's offering. And everyone with whom was found acacia wood for any work of the service, brought it. ²⁵ All the women who were gifted artisans spun yarn with their hands, and brought what they had spun, of blue, purple, and scarlet, and fine linen. ²⁶ And all the women whose hearts stirred with wisdom spun yarn of goats' hair. ²⁷ The rulers brought onyx stones, and the stones to be set in the ephod and in the breastplate, ²⁸ and spices and oil for the light, for the anointing oil, and for the sweet incense. ²⁹ The children of Israel brought a freewill offering to the Lord, all the men and women whose hearts were willing to bring material for all kinds of work which the Lord, by the hand of Moses, had commanded to be done.

³⁰ And Moses said to the children of Israel, "See, the Lord has called by name Bezalel the son of Uri, the son of Hur, of the tribe of Judah; ³¹ and He has filled him with the Spirit of God, in wisdom and understanding, in knowledge and all manner of workmanship, ³² to design artistic works, to work in gold and silver and bronze, ³³ in cutting jewels for setting, in carving wood, and to work in all manner of artistic workmanship.

³⁴ "And He has put in his heart the ability to teach, in him and Aholiab the son of Ahisamach, of the tribe of Dan. ³⁵ He has filled them with skill to do all manner of work of the engraver and the designer and the tapestry maker, in blue, purple, and scarlet thread, and fine linen, and of the weaver—those who do every work and those who design artistic works."
(Exodus 35:1- 35)

God has given ability and skill to this community but we are treating them as a low caste. It seems necessary to improve our Christian society to treat the community. The original language of Nepal is *Charmakar* (tanner), not Sarki.

"Also, for Adam and his wife, the Lord God made tunics of skin, and clothed them." (Genesis 3:21)

God himself is a tanner.

In those days, John the Baptist came preaching in the wilderness of Judea, ² and saying, "Repent, for the kingdom of heaven is at hand!" ³ For this is he who was spoken of by the prophet Isaiah, saying, "The voice of one crying in the wilderness, 'Prepare the way of the Lord; make His paths straight.'" ⁴ Now John himself was clothed in camel's hair, with a leather belt around his waist; and his food was locusts and wild honey. (Matthew 3:1-4)

John the Baptist was also a tanner. He has made a camel's hair jacket by himself and tied his waist with a leather belt that he made himself.

So it was that he stayed many days in Joppa with Simon, a tanner. (Acts 9:43)

Send therefore to Joppa and call Simon here, whose surname is Peter. He is lodging in the house of Simon, a tanner, by the sea. When he comes, he will speak to you.' (Acts 10:32) Here also Simon Peter was a tanner and Paul was also a tanner. For Paul also made and sold leather tents. Peter and Paul were also tanners.

How do we take the teachings of Paul and Peter? Are they both low caste people?

HOW DID THE BIBLE BEGIN?

1. Papyrus started from the skin of a wild tree. From Egypt and Syria, the word of the Bible was transferred to it from the Byblos tree.

2. It was written in red ink after extracting skins from sheep, goats, and deer.

You and I have God's Word in our hands. If the tanners had not written the Bible with such hard work, we would not have had the opportunity to know God today and would not have had the opportunity to study His Word. The passage of the Bible mentioned below proves that the word of the Bible was first written on skin and will be on parchment in the end times.

And I saw in the right hand of Him who sat on the throne a scroll written inside and on the back, sealed with seven seals. ² Then, I saw a strong angel proclaiming with a loud voice, "Who is worthy to open the scroll and to loose its seals?" ³And no one in heaven or on the earth or under the earth was able to open the scroll, or to look at it.

⁴ So I wept much, because no one was found worthy to open and read the scroll, or to look at it. ⁵ But one of the elders said to me, "Do not weep. Behold, the Lion of the tribe of Judah, the Root of David, has prevailed to open the scroll and to loose its seven seals."

⁶ And I looked, and behold, in the midst of the throne and of the four living creatures, and in the midst of the elders, stood a Lamb as though it had been slain, having seven horns and seven eyes, which are the seven Spirits of God sent out into all the earth. (Revelation 5:1-6)

I saw still another mighty angel coming down from heaven, clothed with a cloud. And a rainbow was on his head, his face was like the sun, and his feet like pillars of fire. ² He had a little book open in his hand. And he set his right foot on the sea and his left foot on the land, ³ and cried with a loud voice, as when a lion roars. When he cried out, seven thunders uttered their voices. ⁴ Now when the seven thunders uttered their voices, I was about to write; but I heard a voice from heaven saying to me, "Seal up the things which the seven thunders uttered, and do not write them."

⁵ The angel whom I saw standing on the sea and on the land raised up his hand to heaven ⁶ and swore by Him who lives forever and ever, who created heaven and the things that are in it, the earth and the things that are in it, and the sea and the things that are in it, that there should be delay no longer, ⁷ but in the days of the sounding of the seventh angel, when he is about to sound, the mystery of God would be finished, as He declared to His servants the prophets.

⁸ Then, the voice which I heard from heaven spoke to me again and said, "Go, take the little book which is open in the hand of the angel who stands on the sea and on the earth." ⁹ So I went to the angel and said to him, "Give me the little book." And he said to me, "Take and eat it; and it will make your stomach bitter, but it will be as sweet as honey in your mouth."[10] *Then I took the little book out of the angel's hand and ate it, and it was as sweet as honey in my mouth. But when I had eaten it, my stomach became bitter. (Revelation 10:1-10)*

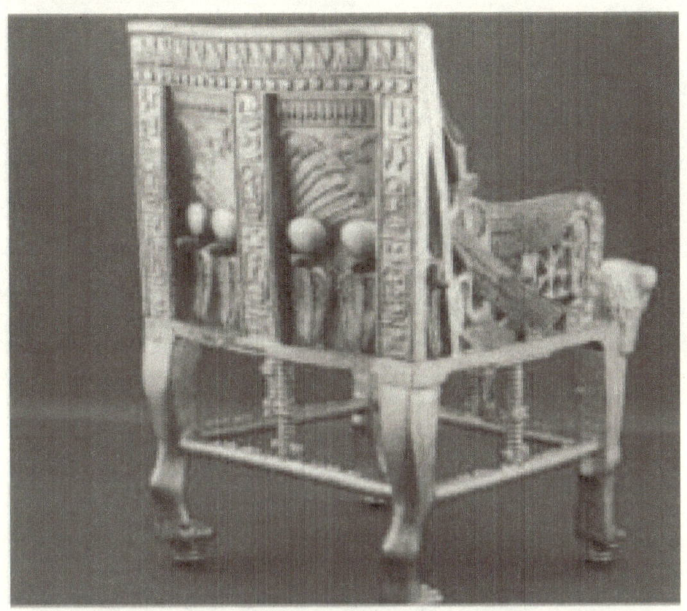

The throne of the King Pharoah and hidden cobra

The throne of the King of Nepal

Bird and cobra in the Crown of Egypt

Symbolic bird and cobra in the Crown of Nepal

Snake as in the crown of the Pharoah

King Pharoah

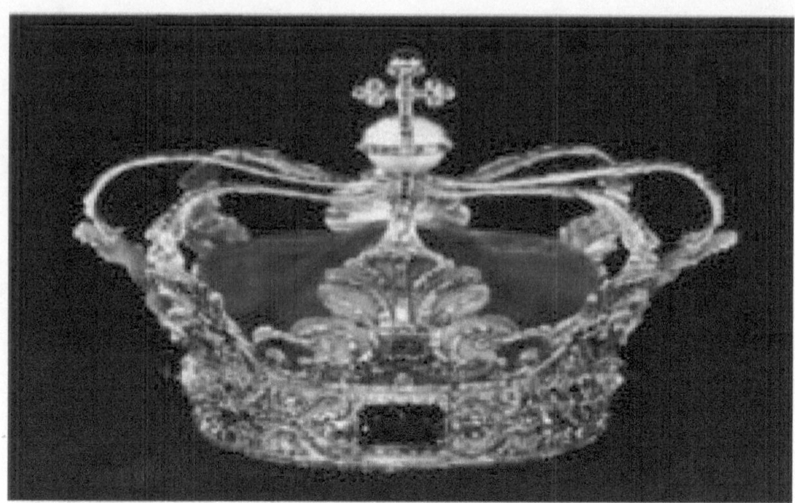

Crown of the monarchs

Statue of the King of Egypt

Chapter 5

Aryan History

Aryan Brahmins look dangerous and clever in the world. They talk about non-violence by being confrontational but do not allow open confrontation. These are the same people who killed Gandhi and consider themselves Gandhians in the world. There are two types of well-known anti-humans in the world. The difference is that Zionists have always maintained their identity. We can look at history about who they are and who anti-Jews are. About six million Jews were killed during Hitler's time and Aryan's kingdom planned to take over the world.

A mysterious sign and symbol was erected and the Swastika symbol or flag was created to demonstrate the identity and power of the German Aryans. The people of Europe are fully aware of this sign and are taught about it. What does a sign do? We may think that way. But its mysterious meaning is to eliminate the entire community other than the Aryans.

(Bible Yatra, p. 232, Author Balkumari)

In another writer B.P. Koirala's literary work *Hitler and the Jews* it is written on page 111, "Hitler, you could not say anything in response to inhuman brutality?" Hitler says "I am not cruel at all. Cruelty is escapism - the impulsive action from which I consider myself free. In fact, I am also free from pity, because pity is also a dominant emotion, so I have abandoned it like poison."

Hitler, don't you have a conscience? (p.113)

No, it is a clever Jewish invention.

BP Koirala says on page 119, "I spent only a few weeks in Germany, not many days. But I felt that I was returning to my country after spending an era there. However, since leaving London, I had already left for my country. But it was only after I left Hanover that I felt that my journey abroad was over. Now, I was really oriented towards my home. The German land had begun to fade in the twilight.

The passenger sitting next to my seat did not say anything for a moment. Once, he got up and pulled a portmanteau from the rack above. He took out a small book from it and put it in his pocket on the back of the seat in front of him. He put the wagon back on the rack and sat back in his seat in preparation for the journey. I took one quick look at him and then started to look at the German coming down. However, it was a simple courtesy of an Indian traveller.

But I was probably so immersed in my feelings that when he said, "Hello," I started looking at him with a start and after a moment I replied, "Hello." He said, "You are not Hindustani too?" "Sir," I said, "I am Nepali." He laughed and said, "You must be very legal."

After all, what is the difference between Hindustan and Nepal? We have the same landscape, same culture, and same history. I said, "But Nepal has a different political existence." "Ah, that is the side effect of British imperialist policy. If they had wanted, they would have broken it into countless pieces."

With a slight arching of his wide and well-stitched Kashmiri coat, he turned towards me and extended his right hand in front of me, palm facing up, and said, "Come, you Nepali and Bengali, brothers and sisters of the same cultural family, shake hands."

I was never used to being in such an enthusiastic friendship, and it was very awkward for me to be in the position of shaking hands at the first stage of the meeting. I looked at him at once and there was a look of openness and confidence on his face. A round face, cheerful black-framed glasses, thin, golden-rod eyes, bright with gaiety, all combined to form the impression of his face, with an outstretched hand of openness, happiness, and warmth, he said, "My name is Dr Sunil Bhattacharya." I took his hand and said, "I am Vishweshwar Prasad Koirala." Dr Sunil Bhattacharya says, "Sir, never think of yourself as an Indian. An integral family—Nepali and Indian."

In my state of mind, with the experience of Hanover and Berlin, if someone had asked me to stay with the family, I would have accepted it without hesitation. I said without speeding up the expression and words, "I am not bound by national boundaries. To tell the truth, when I was traveling in Germany for a few days, my heart was able to establish harmony with the German nation."

He welcomed this simple-hearted humanity of mine so fiercely that I was stunned. Without caring about the other passengers of the ship, he gave a single blow to my bum and said in a loud voice, "what a historical truth! your words sound like a very lost old man's speech. Aryan caste sound…" I started looking at him in amazement. He said that I also believe the same.

There is a great similarity between the German race and the Indian race. Be that as it may, both of them are preserving the memory of the geographical Aryan race in their culture. History is proof of this; we find caste, witnessing it in its footsteps. I took it from *Hitler and the Jews* by Vishweshwar Prasad Koirala's book page no. 119. Hitler's Swastika symbol is considered a sign of good fortune for Aryan society, but for other societies, this symbol is considered as a destructive invisible force.

Of course, *jatjati* means caste in English. In countries outside Nepal and India, jat or caste is neither read nor heard or spoken, but Nepalese leaders, pundits, professors in various bodies, and Christian priests like to pronounce caste.

However, our study of Vishweshwar Prasad Koirala's book shows that in German Aryan and in India as well as in Nepal this symbol (symbol of swastika) is considered a religious and auspicious symbol, but the inner secret is that it is Hitler's symbol of his sole power and rule, and he killed six million Jews and other people with this symbol.

Now the youth generation sees this sign as a curse in Germany. Despite trying to forget, atheists with this swastika symbol are often seen as harsh and cruel people.

In India and Nepal, this symbol is often kept knowingly or unknowingly in religious places and monasteries and often at home as a religious and blessing sign. Its inner secret is to build its own single state and destroy other communities. The reason I have to write this is because this sign is not a sign of Nepal, but a sign of a brutal German Hitler. When we study more intensively, we have been hearing about four castes, thirty-six people since Prithvi Narayan Shah. We hear it from the mother's womb, and such a root is deeply rooted in the family and society, in the mother's womb, in the family, in the community, in the neighbourhood, in the school, in the college, in the workshop, in the administration, in the religious monastery, in the politicians, and in religious leaders. Do not misunderstand that this is a disease not only in the people of Nepal but also in India and Indians as well as in India and Nepal and every breathing person.

Above, we mentioned that Vishweshwar Prasad Koirala has also spoken about caste many times. A strong and powerful leader of the country in language, science, and literature as well as a sensible leader known as a patriot, has mentioned more about Gita, a Hindu scripture, than the value of humanity and authority. (p.126).

Even in page no. 121 it is understood that Markash was an inspired ethnic group. In my opinion, I see that he fought for his sovereignty and nationality and reached the peak through various difficulties. It is not ethnic, but nationalism and patriotism. Seeing such a powerful leader speaking word for word about the Gita and caste, it seems like putting salty, sour poison in the wounds of the Nepalese people.

(In the book of Dr B. P. Khanal, the author of *Distinct Thoughts*, the idea that the conflict between the Christian church and the wall should be improved has been revealed. (p. 277)

The area that the Nepali Christian community should be careful about when talking about the federal form is the caste structure that has emerged in the background of the Hindu Vanarashram here. Due to the same caste social system, no matter how much we emphasize Christian brotherhood, even within the church, our people are affected by the inhuman touch and unjust history that they have experienced till now.

Even today, when the issue of caste is brought out, the hearts of the majority of the people are deeply hurt. Dr B.P. Khanal's next Switzerland visit has been told very well. (*Distinct Thoughts,* p. 282)

Just as in Nepal, King Prithvi Narayan Shah unified the small states that were scattered under different names and places under the power, in the same way, the then Soviet Russia was formed by the tsar ruler there by attacking the neighbouring independent states and forming a single state. Therefore, after the October revolution of 1917, the basis of federalism was decided with the aim of guaranteeing equality to all races. However, Lenin tried to address what he called "class in place of race."

In the same way, although different races have their own specific identities in Switzerland, the framework of federalism is established on the basis of the main language. Especially the people who speak French, German, Italian, and Roman languages, regardless of where they live, have been given rights proportionally to the language population, and the union has been created. But looking at the form of the federal state, Germany is different from other countries. There, Hitler's campaign to accept the existence of only one race as a whole reinforced the concept of Germans being one. They are considered to be people of the same ethnic background who speak the same language. However, there is still geographical and administrative federalism. After a short assessment of the basis of federalism in other countries, we should discuss which basis should be accepted in Nepal. Considering all the above remarkable ideas and visions, I have the opportunity to be more enthusiastic and I am thankful to Dr B.P. Khanal.

I myself have been living in Europe since December 1, 1990. While doing research on European theology after living and visiting different countries, I did not know that caste was ever inquired about anywhere in Europe. I did not even know that caste was asked when entering from one country to another. In many places outside Nepal, it is customary to give your identity in this way, based on nationality and not ethnicity or caste.

If they are from Germany, when they present their identity, they say it like this, "I am German." If you are from Switzerland, "I am Swiss." If I belong to the country of Israel, they say, "I am a Jew." But I have never heard of someone describing themselves as a Jew caste.

But in the context of Nepal, the nationality of a person born in Nepal is Nepali and as a Nepali citizen, he has the right and custom to write Nepali in his citizenship and passport. But in Nepali's understanding, because a person was born in Nepal, I do not have any other surname regarding the universal rights of my country. If I identify myself as a Nepali, they think that this is a small caste and show low behaviour. For example, the best man would be a Nepali small caste, who gives his identity by appreciating and respecting the nationality of Nepal. The best man Nepal respects and respects another as a great caste. Can Nepali be kept in citizenship-based identity? We will return to the topic again, as we read above.

Just as Lenin fought for his caste (people), caste is not understood as caste, but people. Patriots have taken steps for the nation, citizens, and their country by adopting different paths. Hitler also took steps not for caste but for the state and country, although he was totally misled.

Now, we will study Switzerland a little bit. Even in Switzerland, the kings ruled in a small group, but it is not a state like Nepal. Perhaps the chief or the main people kept the group safe.

1291, Habsburger

The princes of the Austrian royal family had to pass through the Suisse Mountain (from Lucerne to Gorthat) for trade to Italy, where bandits had taken over.

1273, Rudolph of the royal family of Germany was a dangerous king. This community lived around it, which is now the centre.

King Rudolph died on July 15, 1291. After the time of King Rudolph, these three communities (Schwyz, Uri, Unterwalden) came together and signed a treaty. Let us help each other's community and we will keep within our circle the invaders from outside and the people who create strife and conflict from within. After making such a treaty, the Habsburger Bern conquered the above Morgatens.

The Habsburgers were members of the royal family of Austria. Even then there was an attack. A verbal agreement was made in the name of God that between the three communities we will be like brothers and not fight and develop our country. Now, the first day of August is celebrated as Swiss National Victory Day.

Walter Furst, URI

Werner Stauffacher, Schwyz

Arnold von Melchtali unterwalden Rutliwiese made a covenant with God forever in the name of Jesus Christ on 1 August 1291. It is written in the covenant, "We will be like brothers of the same family. No attack and invasion will separate us. We will be and remain free like our ancestors before us. We are and will be ready to die rather than be slaves to anyone. We will trust in the mighty God. We will not be afraid of man and the power of the enemy."

(Shweiz Horizont, ISBN 978-3-8003, pp. 102+103 and 1719-6)

As we have studied the historical facts above, it seems necessary to pay attention to two things.

Class system is different and it is related to education, business, and family. But the caste system is different.

On the one hand, intellectual leaders campaign that the caste system should be abolished, for example, Vishweshwar Prasad Koirala is mentioned above.

On the other hand, religious scholars mentioned that no book is being written about caste the system in Europe without any basis. We see Suez caste (people) and German caste (people). I have studied so far and according to my experience, it does not match with regard to the Nepali caste system, instead, another confusion is created in Nepali society.

Another Brahmin community from a pagan background would convert to Christianity to eradicate the caste system and carry out revolutionary actions instead of hiding in the houses of untouchables and eating food at night. The untouchables were invited to their homes without fear of their mothers, fathers, and families. They took them to the kitchen to have a feast and started mixed marriages in the family. Is it because of the fear of the father, mother, and society that he said he hid in the untouchable's house and ate?

If we are aware, will our Pundit father and mother become a role model by calling the untouchables and serving food without fear? If a father is afraid of the mother's fear and society's fear, will he walk without getting full salvation?

We have dreamed of Switzerland, the paradise of the world. We hand over our Nepal to the God who blesses the Swiss, we pray that all four communities are brothers and if we make a covenant, surely our country will become not only the most beautiful country in the world but also the most blessed country in the world. Christianity began in Asia. The people of Asia were very wise and chased the Christians. Switzerland was blessed with faith after the gospel of Jesus reached Europe. Blessings and development are needed, but what to do with springs and resources?

In my opinion, if all four communities work together to develop the country without discriminating against each other, big countries cannot attack us. We have dreamed of making a developed country like Switzerland and we have also made plans, but until our hearts and minds change, there can be no radical change in the country. The king of Switzerland is Jesus and the national flag of that country has a cross; its national anthem contains words of Christian worship, which song is sung in a poetic style. The Constitution is written on a biblical basis.

Wikipedia 'Rutlischwar' English ruth Dath

Chapter 6
Law of Religion

The Halakhah Bible tells us what a good life is, and one that is full of knowing and doing what should be done. For example, Exodus 18:20 says, "And you shall teach them the statutes and the laws, and show them the way in which they must walk and the work they must do."

The Talmud (Shab 138b) also calls "the word of God" halakhah according to Amos 8:12. According to the rabbinic saying, after the destruction, God has nothing to do but four hands (ala khan Ber M 8a). The Talmuds Tosefta Sifra and Sifrei also say that Moses, the teacher, on Mount Sinai, explained to the people from his own mouth all the acceptable and forbidden, holy and impure work, duties and obligations, worthy and unworthy. According to the traditional thinking of halakhic Judaism, "Written laws are not legal, religious, moral compilations or come from different sources but are the nature and essence and the revealed will of God (historical event shown at Mount Sinai). These rules are considered as commandments: positive and negative (See Commandments, the 613). Not everything can come in the interpretation of the laws of the Torah. From a classical point of view, Nahmanides' statement on principal Maimories Sefer haMityrot and his variations seem to be correct. The interpretation of the prophets and Hagiographa was considered a commandment and a forbidding commandment. They often explained the Torah. Traditionally, they used to make it an oral law.

THE ORAL LAW

Oral laws include laws transmitted in writing that have been interpreted and analyzed by sages. All the small details on Mount Sinai are examples of prohibitions and logical deductions given to Moses at Sinai.

INTERPRETATION OF THE WRITTEN LAW

However, according to the accepted hermeneutical rules, the analysis of the Bible text is expressed. According to Talmudic tradition, anything that has been transmitted directly from the tradition is counted/recognized as de orayta. It is considered as the written law in daily life. Rather, the halakhah has a different view of the context. Because the Talmud does not have its own classical dogma system on this matter.

Maimonides and Nahmanides differ from this. According to Maimonides (seferha-Mitzvot, principle 2) anything is de-orayta if it is explained and analyzed. But it should be recognized by the world and tradition. If the Talmud itself cannot prove transmission, then it is de-rabbanan or the words or the *soferim* (Sefaria Edition 2021).

LOGICAL DEDUCTION

Sometimes, the authors of the Talmud say that 'any halakhah is self-authenticating.' Since the scriptures themselves are axiomatic, no other evidence is needed. Before a person declares something, he has to prove it, but the scriptures do not need to be proved by other things.

Basic ideas such as hazakah, the main rule, etc., are intended to support halakhah by theological texts. The verses themselves are not sources but intellectual logic and equality.

SAYING OR THE SCRIBES (ELDERS)

According to the sentence of the law in which they instruct you, according to the judgment which they tell you, you shall do; you shall not turn aside to the right hand or to the left from the sentence which they pronounce upon you. (Deuteronomy 17:11)

Deuteronomy 17:11 says that it is good to obey the commandments of bet din. Not in the Torah, but in its entirety, where it can be applied, it should be applied and those who do not agree to follow it are warned. (p. 6/15 Custom)

There are various meanings/definitions of "custom" (in Hebrew Minhab) in Talmudic literature. All of them are considered as sources of halakhah, but not all of them have the same force.

Where halakhah is not clear, religious custom is relied upon. "Every halakhah that is not clear in the bet din and if you do not know its tendency, go to the community, observe how the community operates, and act accordingly." (TJ Pc'ah 7:5). Here, the concept of custom is close to the concept of consensus in Muslim law, especially when looking at their original stage. Humans are not completely err, so matter is decided on the basis of custom. Its nature is the nature of halakhah.

The Babylonian Talmud expresses this idea in this way, "Go and see how the nations/people are accustomed to the rules/laws/work." (Ber. 45a). Hillel clarifies definitively and says, "Leave all these to Israel. If they are not prophets, then they are the children of the Prophet." (Pes. 66a). pp. 11/15

By strengthening the dominance of Babylonian education politically, Baghdad became the seat of a Caliphate. pp. 11/15

TALMUDIC LAW

Takkanah had the potential to deal with new situations that Talmudic law could not cover.

CODIFICATION OR THE HALAKHAH

The teachers of halakhah were of two types during the middle ages and later. At first, there were two types of legal theorists: Rashi and tosafists. Their main work was to expound the classical laws of the Talmud and early rabbinic writings.

HALAKHAH

The Bible says that a good person is one who knows what he should do and does what he should do. For example, Exodus 18:20 says, "And you shall teach them the statutes and the laws, and show them the way in which they must walk and the work they must do."

The Talmud (Shab 138b) also calls "the word of God" halakhah according to Amos 8:12 which says, "They shall wander from sea to sea, and from north to east; they shall run to and fro, seeking the word of the Lord, but shall not find it."

According to the rabbinic saying, after the destruction, God has nothing to do but four hands (halakhah beri: 8a).

The Talmuds Tosefta Sifra and Sifrei also say that Moses, the teacher, on Mount Sinai, explained to the people from his own mouth all the acceptable and forbidden, holy and impure work, duties and obligations, worthy and unworthy.

According to the traditional thinking of halakhic Judaism, written laws are not legal, religious, moral compilations or come from different sources but are the nature and essence and the revealed will of God (historical event shown at Mount Sinai). These rules are considered as commandments: positive and negative (See Commandments, the 613).

Not everything can come in the interpretation of the laws of the Torah. From a classical point of view, Nahmanides' statement on principal Maimories Sefer ha_Mityrot and his variations seem to be correct.

The interpretation of the prophets and Hagiographa was considered a commandment and a forbidding commandment.

They often explained the Torah. Traditionally, they used to make it an oral law.

THE ORAL LAW

Oral laws include laws transmitted in writing that have been interpreted and analyzed by sages.

All the small details on Mount Sinai are examples of prohibitions and logical deductions given to Moses at Sinai.

INTERPRETATION OF THE WRITTEN LAW

However, according to the accepted hermeneutical rules, the analysis of the Bible text is expressed. According to Talmudic tradition, anything that has been transmitted directly from the tradition is counted/recognized as de-orayta.

It is considered as the written law in daily life. Rather, the halakhah has a different view of the context. Because the Talmud does not have its own classical dogma system on this matter.

Maimonides and Nahmanides differ from this. Sometimes, the authors of the Talmud say that 'any halakhah is self-authenticating.'

Since the scriptures themselves are axiomatic, no other evidence is needed. Before a person declares something, he has to prove it, but the scriptures do not need to be proved by other things.

Basic ideas such as hazakah, the main rule, etc., are intended to support halakhah by theological texts. The verses themselves are not sources but intellectual logic and equality.

According to the sentence of the law in which they instruct you, according to the judgment which they tell you, you shall do; you shall not turn aside to the right hand or to the left from the sentence which they pronounce upon you. (Deuteronomy 17:11)

Deuteronomy 17:11 says that it is good to obey the commandments of bet din.

Not in the Torah, but in its entirety, where it can be applied, it should be applied and those who do not agree to follow it, are warned. (p. 9. 6/15 Custom)

There are various meanings/definitions of "custom" (in Hebrew Minhab) in Talmudic literature. All of them are considered as sources of halakhah, but not all of them have the same force.

Where halakhah is not clear, religious custom is relied upon.

"Every halakhah that is not clear in the bet din and if you do not know its tendency, go to the community, observe how the community operates, and act accordingly." (TJ Pc'ah 7:5). Here, the concept of custom is close to the concept of consensus in Muslim law, especially when looking at their original stage. Humans do not completely err. So, matter is decided on the basis of custom. Its nature is the nature of halakhah.

The Babylonian Talmud expresses this idea in this way, "Go and see how the nations/people are accustomed to the rules/laws/work." (Ber. 45a).

Hillel clarifies definitively and says "Leave all these to Israel. If they are not prophets, then they are the children of the Prophet." (Pes. 66a, pp. 11/15)

By strengthening the dominance of Babylonian education politically, Baghdad became the seat of a Caliphate. (pp. 11/15)

Takkanah had the potential to deal with new situations that Talmudic law could not cover.

CODIFICATION OR THE HALAKHAH

The teachers of halakhah were of two types during the middle age and later. At first, there were two types of legal theorists: Rashi and tosafists. Their main work was to expound the classical laws of the Talmud and early rabbinic writings. No matter how much we read about the above Jewish oral, written, practical rules and laws, the practical rules and laws of different communities of Nepal match well. So, when I was looking for where these rules came from, I found them while doing the research. When the Nepali society was stuck in confusion, it was presented with a biblical basis and the meaning and analysis of following the unwritten rules gave clear information to the whole community.

VERBAL RULES OF NEPAL

1. Bible Verses for Sabbath Day of Rest

Then, God blessed the seventh day and sanctified it, because in it He rested from all His work which God had created and made. (Genesis 2:3)

For in six days the Lord made the heavens and the earth, the sea, and all that is in them, and rested the seventh day. Therefore, the Lord blessed the Sabbath day and hallowed it. (Exodus 20:11)

2. Do not touch the dead

And the Lord said to Moses, "Speak to the priests, the sons of Aaron, and say to them: 'None shall defile himself for the dead among his people, except for his relatives who are nearest to him: his mother, his father, his son, his daughter, and his brother.'" (Leviticus 21:1-2)

3. The tail-eating community

4. A community that does not mix milk and meat (Exodus 23:19)

This is the custom in some tailor communities.

5. Festival of First-Fruits

9And the Lord spoke to Moses, saying, 10 "Speak to the children of Israel, and say to them: 'When you come into the land which I give to you, and reap its harvest, then you shall bring a sheaf of the first fruits of your harvest to the priest. 11 He shall wave the sheaf before the Lord, to be accepted on your behalf; on the day after the Sabbath the priest shall wave it. 12 And you shall offer on that day, when you wave the sheaf, a male lamb of the first year, without blemish, as a burnt offering to the Lord. 13 Its grain offering shall be two-tenths of an ephah of fine flour mixed with oil, an offering made by fire to the Lord, for a sweet aroma;

and its drink offering shall be of wine, one-fourth of a hin. [14] You shall eat neither bread nor parched grain nor fresh grain until the same day that you have brought an offering to your God; it shall be a statute forever throughout your generations in all your dwellings. (Leviticus 23:9-14)

There is a custom of eating Nwagi, especially Damai, after harvesting any grain, ask for the first share, and the tailor should be separated before eating. It is customary for the tailor community to take the first portion of fruits and vegetables before eating them, or they come to take the heads.

SABBATICAL YEAR

"Six years you shall sow your land and gather in its produce, but the seventh year you shall let it rest and lie fallow, that the poor of your people may eat; and what they leave, the beasts of the field may eat. In like manner you shall do with your vineyard and your olive grove." (Exodus 23:10-11)

And the Lord spoke to Moses on Mount Sinai, saying, [2] "Speak to the children of Israel, and say to them: 'When you come into the land which I give you, then the land shall keep a Sabbath to the Lord. [3] Six years you shall sow your field, and six years you shall prune your vineyard, and gather its fruit; [4] but in the seventh year there shall be a Sabbath of solemn rest for the land, a Sabbath to the Lord. You shall neither sow your field nor prune your vineyard. [5] What grows of its own accord of your harvest you shall not reap, nor gather the grapes of your untended vine, for it is a year of rest for the land. [6] And the Sabbath produce of the land shall be food for you: for you, your male and female servants, your hired man, and the stranger who dwells with you, [7] for your livestock and the beasts that are in your land—all its produce shall be for food. (Leviticus 25:1-7)

Different communities say about oral laws and rules like this, "Our traditional father and grandfather used to give answers like where it came from, how it came, when it came, why it came, we don't know."

Unwritten customs that have been practiced for generations are also found in the tailor community many years ago people with Nagarchi surnames such as Nyaydhis, Naike, Mukhiya. The people of the Nagarchi surname of this tailor community used to gather seven people once in seven years and take a bath in the morning and fast for seven days without doing any agricultural work and did not talk to neighbours and family. It was customary for all seven people to celebrate the Sabbath year for seven days, but this custom has now disappeared. Perhaps, if you ask the residents of the community more than ninety years of age, there may be a possibility to listen from them. This custom may not be in all the Nagarchi communities. For some information, the expert adviser of King Prithvi Narayan Shah seems to have played two important roles in the success of King Prithvi Narayan Shah's kingdom. It is understood that he had a good practice in the religious laws of the Nagarchi community and was an unlettered expert on God.

That is why Prithvi Narayan won victory over the aboriginal people with the help and advice of Vishe Nagarchi. Another thing is that Bishe Ngarchi may have been a gifted Jew in tailoring. With all the information above, there is no reason why the tailor community is not of Jewish background. The king's clothes were sewn by Bishe Garchi himself as history tells us.

Why didn't the aboriginal people take the tailor community, the community that has been living together with our tribal community since the beginning, as a consultant?

What I mean to say is that if the tailor community had been asked for advice from the Nagarchi community as a political advisor, would the state not have been destroyed by their own hands?

Even now, in our Nepal and India, it is customary for the leaders to keep only the experts of their own factions and communities as advisors, and these are the children of the Bishe Nagarchi. If the tanner community that ran the state and the community that had the engineering gift to destroy the world in India were accepted as advisors, would the country have progressed towards the victory of progress? For more information about Bishe Nagarchi, go to this source and read.

Another evidence is A Sociolinguistic survey among the Nagarchi community in India: NGARCHI COMMUNITY OF CENTRAL INDIA

http://www.sil.org/resources/publication /entry/9044

Urban communities have entered Gondi and Hindi. Nagarchal and Nagarchi are the same. These communities are found in different provinces of India. Their population is around 14 million.

When asked about caste, we say servant of God. They say that they don't know about heaven and hell, they don't have that much information. But they believe in child or supreme, it means child or supreme who believe in the only powerful son of God have been listening orally for thousands of years, but there is a need for someone to tell them about Jesus, the son of God, is the Lord Saviour. The organization called Joshua Project has made a great contribution for people to bring them into Jesus.

SALL AND GANDRA

If you ask about heaven and hell, then where is God? In answer, we can say that the presence of God can be seen towards the hills and mountains. That is why the higher part is considered as a holy mountain.

Since there is no religious rule in writing, many Gonds have entered into Hinduism and entered into an agreement so that they will not suffer any punishment in society. It can be understood that the untouchable community in Nepal used to worship the society by putting on the tika.

Their death is particularly compatible with our aboriginal community of Nepal. For example, if someone dies in the Rai community, it is customary to bury them outside the house in a nearby field. Their belief is that the souls of the dead protect their descendants and stay with them.

Their main food is made from loose millet flour and vegetables, especially dried greens are popular. But sometimes, other foods like lentils, rice, vegetables and other dishes are also used in the kitchen.

They claim that they are aboriginal children from the continent of Australia. About the caste, the government of India has certified it. In 2007, in some provinces of Uttar Pradesh, the government re-designated them as Scheduled Tribes.

They prefer to do farming and consume their own produce. It is understood that they have given great support to the country related to food. In these communities also, the responsibility of their own special personalities is seen in this way.

Management

- Panchayat

- Own boss

- Judge yourself

- Himself is a priest

The tailor community of the past also held similar responsibilities and positions of blowing trumpets.

- The horn of the ram is the beginning of the Israelite horn • Narasinga

- Dholak, Tamko and Damaha are mostly made by themselves and they play Sanahi, Damaha, Narsinga, Trumpet and now some new and new instruments as well.

It is very similar to the tailor community of Nepal. Halakhah proves unwritten.

Gaine (Musician/Singer) community

Adhikari, Kami, Kalalakoushik, Kala, Paudel, Kalichan, Gasai, Jogi, Thakuri, Turki, Bahun, Budhathoki, Baikar, Vagyakaar, Baistha, Bista, Bogte, Bhushal, Bhushalparvate, Maheshwar, Vishwakarma, Vishnupada, Samundri, Shai, Surasaman, Setaparvate, Setichan, Kukchingarana, etc.

Newari Dalit Community

Kasai (Khadgi, Shai, Shahi), Kusule, (Kapali, Darshandhari), Pode, Deula, Pujari, Kuchikar, Dhawi, Kul, Hararu, etc.

Note: Some Dalit castes within the Newar community of Kathmandu Valley have asked not to call themselves Dalits.

Madhesi Dalit Community

Chamar (Rama, Mahara, Mochi, Harijan), Dum, Dom, Gusharu (Sada, Madhouyasada), Jhagad, (Ugau, Uram), Dusadh, (Paswan), Jhagar, (Kachuwa, Kharava, Bakla, Bujira, Bekh, Lakheda), Khatve (Mandal), etc.

Badi Community

Descendant surnames of the Badi communities found in Nepal, although there is no record, based on tradition, 60% of the total population have their own surnames and 40% of the children born from forced internal relationships, although there is no proof yet. According to the custom of confirmation of the father by their ancestors or mothers, the following surnames have been found.

For example: Khati, Rasailithapa, Rasaili Lekali, Chinal, Baral, Thakur, Rana, Kumal, Khadka, Jogi, Bote, Upadhyaya, Rizal, Singh, Shrestha, Paudel, Adhikari, Kami, Damai, Badshah, Khan, Dhital, Niraula, etc.

Note: "Dalit Definition and Caste Schedule" by the National Dalit Commission at the Midwest Regional Workshop Symposium on Magh 3rd and 4th, 2059 in Nepalgunj.

All the above-mentioned surnames inform us that the Brahmin Pundits derived from the surnames of untouchables.

1. First Mongolian community entered Nepal.

2. Then the Untouchable Harijan, God's children entered.

3. Then Pundit Madhav Upadhyay's article revealed the complete secret to us, Aryans have taken some parts of the above surnames. In my opinion, the background of all of our communities is Israel, which was created by the same God. So, let's all embrace each other and start building the country without quarreling.

It is natural for all of us Nepalese to get confused while studying all the above surnames.

Being entangled in this confusion, we all Nepali community are wandering aimlessly like a leaf blown by the wind.

I have mentioned above what I mean, but we will take a leaf of a tree. There are many plants and trees in the forest that blow when the wind comes and the leaves collide with each other and become scurvy. In the same way, we also bump into each other and we abuse each other. They touch each other. Why should one leaf touch another leaf? There is a custom of insulting by questioning this way.

When God created man, by one person, Adam, man came into this world. Then, Eve was created. Their children who were born after that gradually migrated to different countries and reached the corners of the earth. Although the blood is the same, according to wind, water, weather, and geography, the skin is different in the face. This is definitely not our fault.

We should not forget this either. But the children struggled together within her; and she said, "If all is well, why am I like this?" So she went to inquire of the Lord.[23] And the Lord said to her, "Two nations are in your womb, two peoples shall be separated from your body; one people shall be stronger than the other, and the older shall serve the younger." [24] So, when her days were fulfilled for her to give birth, indeed there were twins in her womb. [25] And the first came out red. He was like a hairy garment all over; so they called his name Esau. (Genesis 25:22-25)

These two brothers were born as two types of caste with different faces and different morals. Since the Nepali Bible is translated from the Hindi Bible so caste is written, but in English it is written as TWO NATIONS ARE IN YOUR WOMB. (Genesis 25:22-25)

Of course, God created like this. When we think this way, God seems to be partial and it is normal for us to think this way. If you and I were God, we wouldn't have created like this, but think about it. God's thoughts and our thoughts are different.

"For My thoughts are not your thoughts, nor are your ways my ways," says the Lord. "For as the heavens are higher than the earth, so are my ways higher than your ways, and my thoughts than your thoughts." (Isaiah 55:8-9)

We are not God's advisers either!

[33] Oh, the depth of the riches both of the wisdom and knowledge of God! How unsearchable are His judgments and His ways past finding out! [34] "For who has known the mind of the Lord? Or who has become His counselor?" [35] "Or who has first given to Him and it shall be repaid to him?" [36] For of Him and through Him and to Him are all things, to whom be glory forever. Amen. (Romans 11:33-36)

Whatever it may be, we must give Him glory.

Now, we will go back and discuss the education taught by our ancestors. Most of the Indians and Nepalese have a custom of answering this question when asked about creation. "Well, our Brahma made five types of people. We didn't get it by choice; karma made it so. We all want to be born in a high family, at a high level, but what can we do when

Brahma gave birth to us in this *Shudra*, and very Shudra community." The answer is that we can't get it by choice.

When Brahma created a human being, we do not get the description of a woman. However, my special subject is focused on Nepalese and Nepalese society.

- Brahmin

- Chhetri

- Baisya

- Shudra

- Dalit

Earlier in Nepal, it was customary to say Shudra, Untouchable, but after some time, we often hear the word Dalit. Let's see the explanation of these two types.

Question 1: Who is Chudra?

The Bible gives the definition of Shudra as follows:

[1] *The vision of Obadiah. Thus says the Lord God concerning Edom (We have heard a report from the Lord, and a messenger has been sent among the nations, saying, "Arise, and let us rise up against her for battle"):* [2] *"Behold, I will make you small among the nations; you shall be greatly despised.* [3] *The pride of your heart has deceived you, you who dwell in the clefts of the rock, whose habitation is high; you who say in your heart, 'Who will bring me down to the ground?* [4] *Though you ascend as high as the eagle, and though you set your nest among the stars, from there I will bring you down," says the Lord.* [5] *"If thieves had come to you,*

If robbers by night—Oh, how you will be cut off!—Would they not have stolen till they had enough? If grape-gatherers had come to you, would they not have left some gleanings? [6] *"Oh, how Esau shall be searched out! How his hidden treasures shall be sought after!* All the men in your confederacy shall force you to the border; the men at peace with you shall deceive you* *and prevail against you. Those who eat your bread shall lay a trap for you. No one is aware of it. * [8] *"Will I not in that day," says the Lord, "Even destroy the wise men from Edom, and understanding from the mountains of Esau?" Then your mighty men, O Teman, shall be dismayed, to the end that everyone from the mountains of Esau May be cut off by slaughter.* [10] *"For violence against your brother Jacob, shame shall cover you, and you shall be cut off forever. (Obadiah 1:1-10)*

It is taught in our various places and schools. I will now focus on Chudra.

Thus says the Lord God concerning Edom. Obadiah was a prophet appointed for Judah. He prophesied about God's judgment against Edom. See Introduction.

1. About Edom: The Edomites were the sons of Jacob, southern neighbors of Judah, so they were related to Israel (v. 10), yet that community became enemies of God's people. They often helped foreign armies that attacked Israel. Now in our country too, the children of Jacob's son who are the Harijans are helping those who plan unseen to persecute the children of God as well as the Christians. The meaning of my words is that the Mongolian society, the Christian society and the community that does not worship idols are being attacked in an invisible way.

Because of Edom's long enmity with the Israelites and their hatred for the Israelites, God's wrath would come upon them. The pride of your heart (1) The Edomites lived in rock crevices and in places where there is seaweed. They were arrogant and thought their land was safe and but God would throw them down. (2) Pride leads to self-deception. The Bible teaches that pride comes before a fall (Proverbs 16:18) and makes God your enemy. (Verse 8; James 4:6; 1 Peter 5:5)

As written in verse 10 "For violence against your brother Jacob, shame shall cover you, and you shall be cut off forever."

Who is Shudra? Shudra means interfering with the rights of God's children to do the following things:

- Do not allow a Christian church to be registered

- Don't let the Bible Training Centre be registered

- Considering Christians as third-class citizens or aliens

- Do not give holiday on Good Friday and Christmas

- Keep in unsafe situation for as long as one lives

- Don't give burial place after death

Shudras signifies injustice, tyranny, not giving rights, even robbing given rights. The meaning of chudra is to harass, beat, spit, and shut up others.

The English Bible and the German Bible say small thoughts, low thoughts, short temper, inferior thoughts, oppressing others like this.

In Oxford Dictionary (p. 789) it is explained like this. Now we will move forward with the Dalit issue again.

What is Dalit?

Who is a Dalit?

Now let's go to study: Who is a Dalit?

Dalit is not a thing. If this is the case, then all things and goods made by Dalits should not be used.

We use the animals' Dalit rears. His art is useful. His sweet singing voice is pleasant. A crown made by his hands can be worn on the head. The handicrafts made by him can be admired. The king can rule on the throne by wearing clothes sewn by him. By playing the instrument in auspicious work, the sound of the instrument can destroy the power of darkness with the sound of Nasimha and Damaha. The leather instruments made by him can be played and decorated. Thousands of things the Dalits make are useful to us, but who are not useful?

Dalits are a community. Many years ago, the Israelites lived in Egypt. The king of Egypt was harsh and cruel. His name was Pharaoh.

We can learn a lot from the entire book of Exodus, not just from Exodus 3:6-10.

In Exodus 3:6, it is written, "I am the God of your father—the God of Abraham, the God of Isaac, and the God of Jacob."

In verses 7-8 it is written, "I have surely seen the oppression of my people who are in Egypt, and have heard their cry because of their taskmasters, for I know their sorrows. So, I have come down to deliver them out of the hand of the Egyptians, and to bring them up from that land to a good and large land, to a land flowing with milk and honey, to the place of the Canaanites and the Hittites and the Amorites and the Perizzites and the Hivites and the Jebusites."

In another part of the Bible, it is written like this, "Who executes justice for the oppressed, who gives food to the hungry? The Lord gives freedom to the prisoners. The Lord opens the eyes of the blind; the Lord raises those who are bowed down; the Lord loves the righteous." (Psalm 146:7-8)

ISBN 962327-382-7 CODE 10 NEPA103M

It is written as Dalit in this Bible.

In another Bible (ISBN 978-0-7361-05705) it is written that justice should be done in favour of the oppressed.

Hindi Bible Hindi- O.V.

10G 0066/93-94/15 M PL C35 95 m

ISBN 81-221-1067-3

In the Hindi Bible, it is written *Pise Huo*. In English Bible and German Bible, two languages are found.

ISBN 978-3-417-25990-2 Bestell-NR. 225,990

ISBN 978-3-89436-752-7 Bestell-NR. 273,752

When looking at all the Bibles, it is found that all of them are trying to say the same thing. In Nepali, acronym Dalit means:

Da: beaten, placed under the foot

Li: absorbed, engrossed, single-minded, single-minded

T: it is understood to be destruction and not able to handle.

Many other explanations can be given. I have already given some differences and explanations about Shudra and Dalit above.

Now, we will proceed to distinguish the differences.

1. From the beginning, the Israelites were forbidden to bow down to any idol or image:

And God spoke all these words, saying: 2 "I am the Lord your God, who brought you out of the land of Egypt, out of the house of bondage. 3 "You shall have no other gods before Me. 4 "You shall not make for yourself a carved image—any likeness of anything that is in heaven above, or that is in the earth beneath, or that is in the water under the earth; 5 you shall not bow down to them nor serve them. For I, the Lord your God, am a jealous God, visiting the iniquity of the fathers upon the children to the third and fourth generations of those who hate Me. (Exodus 20:1-5)

In Egypt, under the rule of the cruel pharaoh king, the rights were robbed and they were persecuted according to the above description.

Nepal also has the same regime from the beginning. Even in the crown of our former king, the serpent's head or protector is seen. The same crown has the same rule. Snakes have been a symbol of God's enemies since the beginning. Now, even though there is the rule of the people and not of the king, the Jews and Christians who do not worship idols have been oppressed by a cruel type of rule as the pharaoh did.

Now let's study a little in our native language of Nepal about Shudra. Another word was used in Nepal before Dalit.

What is untouchable? Who is he?

Of course, the word untouchable is neither new nor bad. It's just that the reason why who should not touch whom is not written clearly or our ancestors did not get the opportunity to explain. From the time we are born, our parents give us simple information about what to touch and what not to touch. For example, it is forbidden to touch the smelly and rotten things. For the germs of any disease can be transmitted. But we are taught by our parents from childhood that there are the small caste and the big caste, the holy caste and profane caste. This is a serious malaise within us. I travelled to many countries and sought opportunities to learn from many communities and cultures and people of other languages in order to find out the reason for this and I got it.

For reasons not clearly stated, I had encountered with two people. The lower caste should not touch the higher caste. This custom is common in Nepal and India and with Nepalese living outside of Nepal. For example, even in Israel, Nepal's distant neighbour, this custom has been in place since before, and especially in Israel, God Himself said this after bringing the Jews out of Egypt.

And God spoke all these words, saying, 2 "I am the Lord your God, who brought you out of the land of Egypt, out of the house of bondage." 3 "You shall have no other gods before Me." 4 "You shall not make for yourself a carved image—any likeness of anything that is in heaven above, or that is in the earth beneath, or that is in the water under the earth; 5 you shall not bow down to them nor serve them. For I, the Lord your God, am a jealous God, visiting[c] the iniquity of the fathers upon the children to the third and fourth generations of those who hate Me." (Exodus 20:1-5)

He said not to worship idols and commanded not to bow down, that is why the Jews do not worship idols and do not bow down to work made by hands.

In the New Testament Bible, it is written:

Do not be unequally yoked together with unbelievers. For what fellowship has righteousness with lawlessness? And what communion has light with darkness? 15 And what accord has Christ with Belial? Or what part has a believer with an unbeliever? 16 And what agreement has the temple of God with idols? For you are the temple of the living God. As God has said: "I will dwell in them and walk among them. I will be their God,

And they shall be My people." 17 Therefore "Come out from among them and be separate, says the Lord. Do not touch what is unclean, and I will receive you."18 "I will be a Father to you, and you shall be My sons and daughters, says the Lord Almighty." (2 Corinthians 6:14-18) The Lord God urges the Christian believers to believe in the Lord of the universe, the invisible God whom we cannot see.

Do not be unequally yoked together with unbelievers mean not to marry a non-Christian. The idea of praying and not praying as well as participating in various festivals and rituals leads to compromise. As a result, it is difficult to bring happiness in marriage and after the birth of children it is difficult to guide the child in training and practice.

Any other business and other accounting may not be transparent and problems may arise. Children can be aimless and become restless.

It is questioned in verse 15, "What accord has Christ with Belial?" Belial is devil, Satan and Lucifer. We don't have any agreement with him and his works.

In verse 16, it said that what agreement has the temple of God with idols? Because we are temples of the living God as God said.

I will dwell in them and walk among them. I will be their God, and they shall be my people.

This verse calls us to come out of the unholy culture.

"Therefore, come out from among them and be separate," says the Lord. "Do not touch what is unclean, and I will receive you…"

If you look closely at the secret in this verse, in the Nepali context, those who worship idols touch those who do not worship idols. It proves that idolatry is impure and the people and communities who worship idols are impure and untouchable. In our Nepali society, the earlier aboriginal people used to perform ancestor worship.

Ancestor-worshippers

God is also inviting the ancestor worshippers, giving them the opportunity to go out and worship Him.

The worshipping community means (Damai, Kami, Sarki) Syojikar, Vishwakarma, Charamkar community.

These same communities were commanded by God Himself not to worship idols and be obeyed in Exodus 20:1-5. Especially these communities are not untouchables, because they are a holy caste that does not worship idols. Our Aryan community is in Nepal. Especially Aryan community should not touch the worshiping community because they are worshipers of Baal deity from the beginning. But in the context of the Nepali, the interpretation was not in this way but in another way.

We see in the above Nepali festivals, rituals, customs, business, and professional divisions. But where did the religious system in Nepal come from?

And the Lord spoke to Moses, saying, [2] "Speak to the children of Israel, and say to them: 'The feasts of the Lord, which you shall proclaim to be holy convocations, these are My feasts. [3] 'Six days shall work be done, but the seventh day is a Sabbath of solemn rest, a holy convocation. You shall do no work on it; it is the Sabbath of the Lord in all your dwellings. (Leviticus 23:1-3)

The Lord spoke to Moses, saying, "The feasts of the Lord, which you shall proclaim to be holy convocations, these are my feasts."

SABBATH-DAY

[9]*And the Lord spoke to Moses, saying,* [10] *"Speak to the children of Israel, and say to them: 'When you come into the land which I give to you, and reap its harvest, then you shall bring a sheaf of the first fruits of your harvest to the priest.* [11] *He shall wave the sheaf before the Lord, to be accepted on your behalf; on the day after the Sabbath the priest shall wave it.* [12] *And you shall offer on that day, when you wave the sheaf, a male lamb of the first*

year, without blemish, as a burnt offering to the Lord. [13] Its grain offering shall be two-tenths of an ephah of fine flour mixed with oil, an offering made by fire to the Lord, for a sweet aroma; and its drink offering shall be of wine, one-fourth of a hin. [14] You shall eat neither bread nor parched grain nor fresh grain until the same day that you have brought an offering to your God; it shall be a statute forever throughout your generations in all your dwellings. (Leviticus 23:9-14)

"It shall be, in regard to their inheritance, that I am their inheritance. You shall give them no possession in Israel, for I am their possession. (Ezekiel 44:28)

Honour the Lord with your possessions, And with the first fruits of all your increase; (Proverbs 3:9)

A sheaf of the first harvest of the crop, the feast of the first fruits, identifies the growth of the land as coming from the Lord. In Nepal, especially on this day, two communities (priest and tailor community) get share or part. There is the special tradition in the village houses.

"When you reap the harvest of your land, you shall not wholly reap the corners of your field when you reap, nor shall you gather any gleaning from your harvest. You shall leave them for the poor and for the stranger: I am the Lord your God." (Leviticus 23:22)

There was such a custom in the mountains of Nepal too.

[23] Then the Lord spoke to Moses, saying, [24] "Speak to the children of Israel, saying: 'In the seventh month, on the first day of the month, you shall have a Sabbath-rest, a memorial of blowing of trumpets, a holy convocation. [25] You shall do no customary work on it; and you shall offer an offering made by fire to the Lord.'" (Leviticus 23:23-25)

On the special day of the start of Dashain, it was customary for Damais to play Narsimha or *Sanahi* on the hill and always play it in the evening from house to house to give a signal or notice that Dashain has arrived. It was also popular in village houses but it is gradually disappearing.

FOUR KINDS OF SACRIFICIAL PRACTICES

- Bada Dashain

- Chaitya Dashai

- Bhimsen Puja in November-December

- Bhimsen Puja in April-May

It can be assumed that the custom of celebrating Holi started from India. In the Islamic society, it is customary to torture the body by beating the body and drawing blood. Although it seems strange to look at this, it can be assumed that the deeper meaning of the red colour in the Holi is to purify the blood of the Lord Jesus.

DAY OF ATONEMENT

And the priest, who is anointed and consecrated to minister as priest in his father's place, shall make atonement, and put on the linen clothes, the holy garments; [33] then he shall make atonement for the Holy Sanctuary, and he shall make atonement for the tabernacle of meeting and for the altar, and he shall make atonement for the priests and for all the people of the assembly. (Leviticus 16:32-33)

Different places in Nepal have their own priests in different communities. They bathe in the morning and wear special white clothes. This means that the elder, mature and strong person of the family carries the load. In particular, two sacrificial animals are mentioned in the Bible. The rich sacrifice two pure, unblemished lamb or goat or pig according to their ability. Those who are unable to offer two sacrifices, decorate the place of sacrifice with cucumber and ash pumpkin in the yard. First, the priest or the head of the house transfers everyone's sins to goats or animals with both water. Then, the priest cuts the cucumber, after that the ash pumpkin, after that the animal. There is a tradition of sprinkling and wiping the blood of the head on the door frame and other materials as well as inside and outside, and with that blood, it is customary to give blood on the forehead to all the members of the family. It should be a blood tika only and it is customary to put it on the forehead.

In the Bible, instead of a bull, a cucumber and ash pumpkin, and a third animal are cut off. This sacrificial festival is considered as Vijayadashami in Nepal. Based on a true story, in Nepal the ten-day festival has been turned into a fictional story of Vijayadashami after another religious battle. But especially in our Nepal, the aborginial Baise and the kingdom of Mongolian Lichchavi Kirants of Chauvise kingdom was eliminated by Prithvi Narayan Shah and the day of victory was named as Vijayadashami.

On the day of the killing of their sons and daughters, our people are supposed to wear ashes and mourn, but they go around drinking alcohol and beating others with a tika on their foreheads.

MAGHE SANKRANTI (TRANSITION OF THE SUN FROM THE ZODIAC OF SAGITTARIUS TO CAPRICORN)

You shall offer up a cake of the first of your ground meal as a heave offering; as a heave offering of the threshing floor, so shall you offer it up. Of the first of your ground meal, you shall give to the Lord a heave offering throughout your generations. (Numbers 15:20-21)

This festival is also celebrated with grandeur in Nepal. This day is known as the day of Thanksgiving in India.

And they journeyed from Elim, and all the congregation of the children of Israel came to the Wilderness of Sin, which is between Elim and Sinai, on the fifteenth day of the second month after they departed from the land of Egypt. [2] Then the whole congregation of the children of Israel complained against Moses and Aaron in the wilderness. [3] And the children of Israel said to them, "Oh, that we had died by the hand of the Lord in the land of Egypt, when we sat by the pots of meat and when we ate bread to the full! For you have brought us out into this wilderness to kill this whole assembly with hunger." (Exodus 16:1-3)

The tradition of letting go of bulls is also found in Nepal, especially in big cities, but it is forbidden to beat them.

A CUSTOM OF RELEASING THE SCAPEGOAT

Then, Aaron shall cast lots for the two goats: one lot for the Lord and the other lot for the scapegoat. (Leviticus 16:8)

Goats and bulls are found around the big temples of Nepal. There is also a popular custom of teasing spoiled boys as Pashupati's bulls and goats in Nepal.

PURANA (HOLY DAYS FOR LISTENING TO SCRIPTURE) CUSTOMS AND ITS MEANING

15 And that they should announce and proclaim in all their cities and in Jerusalem, saying, "Go out to the mountain, and bring olive branches, branches of oil trees, myrtle branches, palm branches, and branches of leafy trees, to make booths, as it is written." 16 Then, the people went out and brought them and made themselves booths, each one on the roof of his house, or in their courtyards or the courts of the house of God, and in the open square of the Water Gate and in the open square of the Gate of Ephraim. 17 So the whole assembly of those who 127 had returned from the captivity made booths and sat under the booths; for since the days of Joshua the son of Nun until that day the children of Israel had not done so. And there was very great gladness. 18 Also day by day, from the first day until the last day, he read from the Book of the Law of God. And they kept the feast seven days; and on the eighth day, there was a sacred assembly, according to the prescribed manner. (Nehemiah 8:15- 18)

Even in Nepal, they do it in the same way when they read seven days of Purana, but they interpret the book based on a story from another Sanskrit book. It is taught by one Pundit for seven days or seven Pundits are invited for one day.

BRONZE BULL STATUE

And King Ahaz cut off the panels of the carts, and removed the lavers from them; and he took down the Sea from the bronze oxen that were under it, and put it on a pavement of stones. (2 Kings 16:17)

Such bull idols are found outside and inside Pashupati as well as all other temples.

ASTHI (BONES RELICS)

Then Joseph took an oath from the children of Israel, saying, "God will surely visit you, and you shall carry up my bones from here." (Genesis 50:25)

And Moses took the bones of Joseph with him, for he had placed the children of Israel under solemn oath, saying, "God will surely visit you, and you shall carry up my bones from here with you." (Exodus 13:19)

The bones of Joseph, which the children of Israel had brought up out of Egypt, they buried at Shechem, in the plot of ground which Jacob had bought from the sons of Hamor, the father of Shechem for one hundred pieces of silver, and which had become an inheritance of the children of Joseph. (Joshua 24:32)

By faith, Joseph, when he was dying, made mention of the departure of the children of Israel, and gave instructions concerning his bones. (Hebrews 11:22) This custom has been going on since very early in Nepal. In case of death in other countries, the relatives of the deceased go to that place to collect ashes.

THE PRACTICE OF LIVING AS A NAZIRITE OR CELIBACY

Then, the Lord spoke to Moses, saying, ² "Speak to the children of Israel, and say to them: 'When either a man or woman consecrates an offering to take the vow of a Nazirite, to separate himself to the Lord, ³ he shall separate himself from wine and similar drink; he shall drink neither vinegar made from wine nor vinegar made from similar drink; neither shall he drink any grape juice, nor eat fresh grapes or raisins. ⁴ All the days of his separation he shall eat nothing that is produced by the grapevine, from seed to skin. ⁵ All the days of the vow of his separation no razor shall come upon his head; until the days are fulfilled for which he separated himself to the Lord, he shall be holy. Then, he shall let the locks of the hair of his head grow. ⁶ All the days that he separates himself to the Lord he shall not go near a dead body. ⁷ He shall not make himself unclean even for his father or his mother, for his brother or his sister, when they die, because his separation to God is on his head. ⁸ All the days of his separation he shall be holy to the Lord. ⁹ And if anyone dies very suddenly beside him, and he defiles his consecrated head, then he shall shave his head on the day of his cleansing; on the seventh day he shall shave it. ¹⁰ Then, on the eighth day, he shall bring two turtledoves or two young pigeons to the priest, to the door of the tabernacle of meeting; ¹¹ and the priest shall offer one as a sin offering and the other as a burnt offering, and make atonement for him, because he sinned in regard to the corpse; and he shall sanctify his head that same day. ¹² He shall consecrate to the Lord the days of his separation, and bring a male lamb in its first year as a trespass offering; but the former days shall be lost, because his separation was defiled. ¹³ Now this is the law of the Nazirite: When the days of his separation are fulfilled, he shall be brought to the door of the tabernacle of meeting. ¹⁴ And he shall present his offering to the Lord: one male lamb in its first year without blemish as a burnt offering, one ewe lamb in its first year without blemish as a sin offering, one ram without blemish as a peace offering, ¹⁵ a basket of unleavened bread, cakes of fine flour mixed with oil, unleavened wafers anointed with oil, and their grain offering with their drink offerings. ¹⁶ Then the priest shall bring them before the Lord and offer his sin offering and his burnt offering; ¹⁷ and he shall offer the ram as a sacrifice of a peace offering to the Lord, with the basket of unleavened bread; the priest shall also offer its grain offering and its drink offering. ¹⁸ Then the Nazirite shall shave his consecrated head at the door of the tabernacle of meeting, and shall take the hair from his consecrated head and put it on the fire which is under the sacrifice of the peace offering. ¹⁹ And the priest shall take the boiled shoulder of the ram, one unleavened cake from the basket, and one unleavened wafer, and put them upon the hands of the Nazirite after he has shaved his consecrated hair; [20] *and the priest shall wave them as a wave offering before the Lord; they are holy for the priest, together with the breast of the wave offering and the thigh of the heave offering. After that, the Nazirite may drink wine.'* [21] *"This is the law of the Nazirite who vows to the Lord the offering for his separation, and besides that, whatever else his hand is able to provide; according to the vow which he takes, so he must do according to the law of his separation." (Numbers 6:1-21)*

Such people are common in Nepal.

THE PRACTICE OF BURNING INCENSE

[46] So Moses said to Aaron, "Take a censer and put fire in it from the altar, put incense on it, and take it quickly to the congregation and make atonement for them; for wrath has gone out from the Lord. The plague has begun." [47] Then Aaron took it as Moses commanded, and ran into the midst of the assembly, and already the plague had begun among the people. So, he put in the incense and made atonement for the people. (Numbers 16:46-47)

This practice is found almost in all places and communities in Nepal. (Read the entire passage from Leviticus 24:1.)

THE CUSTOM OF BINDING PHYLACTERIES AND AMULETS

[6] "And these words which I command you today shall be in your heart. [7] You shall teach them diligently to your children, and shall talk of them when you sit in your house, when you walk by the way, when you lie down, and when you rise up. [8] You shall bind them as a sign on your hand, and they shall be as frontlets between your eyes. (Deuteronomy 6:6-8)

There is a custom of tying the wrists of newly born children in different communities in different places.

EAR PIERCING CUSTOM

Then his master shall bring him to the judges. He shall also bring him to the door, or to the doorpost, and his master shall pierce his ear with an awl; and he shall serve him forever. (Exodus 21:6)

Therefore, the Lord brought upon them the captains of the army of the king of Assyria, who took Manasseh with hooks, bound him with bronze fetters, and carried him off to Babylon. (2 Chronicles 33:11)

Then, you shall take an awl and thrust it through his ear to the door, and he shall be your servant forever. Also to your female servant you shall do likewise. (Deuteronomy 15:17)

Especially, this custom is practiced on children in the Aryan community. Specifically, it means a slave, a servant, under someone's authority. According to Pundit Madhav Prasad's book, the Aryan communities were slaves of Abraham and still have the same signs, characteristics, identity, whether they know it or not, it has a deep meaning.

If we believers also pierce our ears, it means that we are not free or that we are slaves of man. That is why it is better for a faithful boy not to pierce his ears. Although such a practice is fashionable in Christian society, it is a stumbling block for many.

PROHIBITION OF COOKING MEAT AND MILK TOGETHER

The first of the first fruits of your land you shall bring into the house of the Lord your God. You shall not boil a young goat in its mother's milk. (Exodus 23:19)

Especially in the tailor community, this practice is strictly prohibited and they do not prefer or do not eat meat cooked in milk even outside the house.

ABOUT THE TRIDENT

[12]Now the sons of Eli were corrupt; they did not know the Lord. [13]And the priests' custom with the people was that when any man offered a sacrifice, the priest's servant would come with a three-pronged flesh hook [trident] in his hand while the meat was boiling. [14]Then he would thrust it into the pan, or kettle, or caldron, or pot; and the priest would take for himself all that the flesh hook brought up. So, they did in Shiloh to all the Israelites who came there. (1 Samuel 2:12-14)

I don't think there was a trident before this and I didn't see the word trident written in the Bible.

OFFERING MADE BY FIRE

[24]*"Speak to the children of Israel, saying: 'In the seventh month, on the first day of the month, you shall have a Sabbath-rest, a memorial of blowing of trumpets, a holy convocation.* [25] *You shall do no customary work on it; and you shall offer an offering made by fire to the Lord."* [26] *And the Lord spoke to Moses, saying:* [27] *"Also the tenth day of this seventh month shall be the Day of Atonement. It shall be a holy convocation for you; you shall afflict your souls, and offer an offering made by fire to the Lord.* [28] *And you shall do no work on that same day, for it is the Day of Atonement, to make atonement for you before the Lord your God.* [29] *For any person who is not afflicted in soul on that same day shall be cut off from his people.* [30] *And any person who does any work on that same day, that person I will destroy from among his people.* [31] *You shall do no manner of work; it shall be a statute forever throughout your generations in all your dwellings.* (Leviticus 23:24-31)

Such offerings made by fire are found in different places in Nepal. **A NEWLY MARRIED SON SHOULD NOT JOIN THE ARMY**

When a man has taken a new wife, he shall not go out to war or be charged with any business; he shall be free at home for one year, and bring happiness to his wife whom he has taken. (Deuteronomy 24:5) It is applicable in different places in Nepal.

PURIFICATION OF CHILDBIRTH

Then the Lord spoke to Moses, saying, [2] "Speak to the children of Israel, saying: 'If a woman has conceived, and borne a male child, then she shall be unclean seven days; as in the days of her customary impurity she shall be unclean. [3] And on the eighth day the flesh of his foreskin shall be circumcised. [4] She shall then continue in the blood of her purification thirty-three days. She shall not touch any hallowed thing, nor come into the sanctuary until the days of her purification are fulfilled. [5] But if she bears a female child, then she shall be unclean two weeks, as in her customary impurity, and she shall continue in the blood of her purification sixty-six days. [6] When the days of her purification are fulfilled, whether for a son or a daughter, she shall bring to the priest a lamb of the first year as a burnt offering, and a young pigeon or a turtledove as a sin offering, to the door of the tabernacle of meeting. [7] Then he shall offer it before the Lord, and make atonement for her. And she shall be clean from the flow of her blood. This is the law for her who has borne a male or a female. [8] And if she is not able to bring a lamb, then she may bring two turtledoves or two young pigeons—one as a burnt offering and the other as a sin offering. So, the priest shall make atonement for her, and she will be clean.'" (Leviticus 12:1-8)

It is often associated with the Aryan community. Daughters are kept outside in cages or sheds.

PROHIBITIONS ON ILLICIT SEXUAL RELATIONS

Then the Lord spoke to Moses, saying, [2] "Speak to the children of Israel, and say to them: 'I am the Lord your God. [3] According to the doings of the land of Egypt, where you dwelt, you shall not do; and according to the doings of the land of Canaan, where I am bringing you, you shall not do; nor shall you walk in their ordinances. [4] You shall observe My judgments and keep My ordinances, to walk in them: I am the Lord your God. [5] You shall therefore keep My statutes and My judgments, which if a man does, he shall live by them: I am the Lord. [6] None of you shall approach anyone who is near of kin to him, to uncover his nakedness: I am the Lord. [7] The nakedness of your father or the nakedness of your mother you shall not uncover. She is your mother; you shall not uncover her nakedness. [8] *The nakedness of your father's wife you shall not uncover; it is your father's nakedness.* [9] *The nakedness of your sister, the daughter of your father, or the daughter of your mother, whether born at home or elsewhere, their nakedness you shall not uncover.* [10] *The nakedness of your son's daughter or your daughter's daughter, their nakedness you shall not uncover; for theirs is your own nakedness.* [11] *The nakedness of your father's wife's daughter, begotten by your father—she is your sister—you shall not uncover her nakedness.* [12] *You shall not uncover the nakedness of your father's sister; she is near of kin to your father.* [13] *You shall not uncover the nakedness of your mother's sister, for she is near of kin to your mother.* [14] *You shall not uncover the nakedness of your father's brother. You shall not approach his wife; she is your aunt.* [15] *You shall not uncover the nakedness of your daughter-in-law—she is your son's wife—you shall not uncover her nakedness.* [16] *You shall not uncover the nakedness of your brother's wife; it is your brother's nakedness.* [17] *You shall not uncover the nakedness of a woman and her daughter, nor shall you take her son's daughter or her daughter's daughter, to uncover her nakedness. They are near of kin to her. It is wickedness.* [18] *Nor shall you take a woman as a rival to her sister, to uncover her nakedness while the other is alive.* [19] *Also you shall not approach a woman to uncover her nakedness as long as she is in her customary impurity.* [20] *Moreover you shall not lie carnally with your neighbor's wife, to defile yourself with her.* [21] *And you shall not let any of your descendants pass through the fire to Molech, nor shall you profane the name of your God: I am the Lord.* [22] *You shall not lie with a male as with a woman. It is an abomination.* [23] *Nor shall you mate with any animal, to defile yourself with it. Nor shall any woman stand before an animal to mate with it. It is perversion.* [24] *'Do not defile yourselves with any of these things; for by all these the nations are defiled, which I am casting out before you.* [25] *For the land is defiled; therefore, I visit the punishment of its iniquity upon it, and the land vomits out its inhabitants.* [26] *You shall therefore keep My statutes and My judgments, and shall not commit any of these abominations, either any of your own nation or any stranger who dwells among you* [27] *(for all these abominations the men of the land have done, who were before you,* *and thus the land is defiled), * [28] *lest the land vomit you out also when you defile it, as it vomited out the nations that were before you. * [29] *For whoever commits any of these abominations, the persons who commit them shall be cut off from among their people. * [30] *'Therefore you shall keep My ordinance, so that you do not commit any of these abominable customs which were committed before you, and that you do not defile yourselves by them: I am the Lord your God.'" (Leviticus 18:1-30)*

A PRACTICE OF KEEPING THE MUSICIAN COMMUNITY OUTSIDE

[27] *Now at the dedication of the wall of Jerusalem they sought out the Levites in all their places, to bring them to Jerusalem to celebrate the dedication with gladness, both with thanksgivings and singing, with cymbals and stringed instruments and harps. * [28] *And the sons of the singers gathered together from the countryside around Jerusalem, from the villages of the Netophathites, * [29] *from the house of Gilgal, and from the fields of Geba and Azmaveth; for the singers had built themselves villages all around Jerusalem. * [30] *Then the priests and Levites purified themselves, and purified the people, the gates, and the wall.* [31] *So I brought the leaders of Judah up on the wall, and appointed two large thanksgiving choirs. One went to the right hand on the wall toward the Refuse Gate. * [32] *After them went Hoshaiah and half of the leaders of Judah, * [33] *and Azariah, Ezra, Meshullam, * [34] *Judah, Benjamin, Shemaiah, Jeremiah, * [35] *and some of the priests' sons with trumpets—Zechariah the son of Jonathan, the son of Shemaiah, the son of Mattaniah, the son of Michaiah, the son of Zaccur, the son of Asaph, * [36] *and his brethren, Shemaiah, Azarel, Milalai, Gilalai, Maai, Nethanel, Judah, and Hanani, with the musical instruments of David the man of God. And Ezra the scribe went before them. * [37] *By the Fountain Gate, in front of them, they went up the stairs of the City of David, on the stairway of the wall, beyond the house of David, as far as the Water Gate eastward.* [38] *The other thanksgiving choir went the opposite way, and I was behind them with half of the people on the wall, going past the Tower of the Ovens as far as the Broad Wall, * [39] *and above the Gate of Ephraim, above the Old Gate, above*

the Fish Gate, the Tower of Hananel, the Tower of the Hundred, as far as the Sheep Gate; and they stopped by the Gate of the Prison.[40] *So the two thanksgiving choirs stood in the house of God, likewise I and the half of the rulers with me;* [41] *and the priests, Eliakim, Maaseiah, Minjamin, Michaiah, Elioenai, Zechariah, and Hananiah, with trumpets;* [42] *also Maaseiah, Shemaiah, Eleazar, Uzzi, Jehohanan, Malchijah, Elam, and Ezer. The singers sang loudly with Jezrahiah the director.*[43] *Also that day they offered great sacrifices, and rejoiced, for God had made them rejoice with great joy; the women and the children also rejoiced, so that the joy of Jerusalem was heard afar off.*[44] *And at the same time some were appointed over the rooms of the storehouse for the offerings, the first fruits, and the tithes, to gather into them from the fields of the cities the portions specified by the Law for the priests and Levites; for Judah rejoiced over the priests and Levites who ministered.* [45]*Both the singers and the gatekeepers kept the charge of their God and the charge of the purification, according to the command of David and Solomon his son.* [46] *For in the days of David and Asaph of old there were chiefs of the singers, and songs of praise and thanksgiving to God.* [47] *In the days of Zerubbabel and in the days of Nehemiah all Israel gave the portions for the singers and the gatekeepers, a portion for each day. They also consecrated holy things for the Levites, and the Levites consecrated them for the children of Aaron. (Nehemiah 12:27-47)*

There is still a tradition of dancing and singing while going to pick up the bride by playing instruments at weddings in Nepal. Also, these communities are kept outside with instruments in various other auspicious activities of performing Puranas.

SILVER TRUMPETS

And the Lord spoke to Moses, saying: [2] *"Make two silver trumpets for yourself; you shall make them of hammered work; you shall use them for calling the congregation and for directing the movement of the camps.* [3] *When they blow both of them, all the congregation shall gather before you at the door of the tabernacle of meeting.* [4]*But if they blow only one, then the leaders, the heads of the divisions of Israel, shall gather to you.* [5]

When you sound the advance, the camps that lie on the east side shall then begin their journey. ⁶ *When you sound the advance the second time, then the camps that lie on the south side shall begin their journey; they shall sound the call for them to begin their journeys.* ⁷ *And when the assembly is to be gathered together, you shall blow, but not sound the advance.* ⁸ *The sons of Aaron, the priests, shall blow the trumpets; and these shall be to you as an ordinance forever throughout your generations.* ⁹ *"When you go to war in your land against the enemy who oppresses you, then you shall sound an alarm with the trumpets, and you will be remembered before the Lord your God, and you will be saved from your enemies.* ¹⁰ *Also in the day of your gladness, in your appointed feasts, and at the beginning of your months, you shall blow the trumpets over your burnt offerings and over the sacrifices of your peace offerings; and they shall be a memorial for you before your God: I am the Lord your God."* *(Numbers 10:1-10)*

In the past, a separate quota of Damais was opened even within the Nepal Army.

1.   It was customary to play instruments called *Bikule*

2.   Sewing clothes or making army clothes

3.   The tanner community sews shoes as well as prepares various materials

4.   These same communities produce hand weapons as well as other tools and they are found to get involved in Nepal Army, Indian Army, and British Army.

Kirant kings are believed to have ruled for a thousand years. According to Sadhu Kumar Fejong (p. 117) there are 75 generations of Kirant Mundhum history. We also find same in the Bible that there are 75 generations from God to Jesus Christ.

HISTORY OF SHAH DYNASTY

In Nepal, after the end of the kingdom of Licchavi of twenty-five and twenty-six kings, the throne and the crown of the Shah Dynasty are similar to the throne and the crown of the king of Egypt. The serpents sitting as arrows and the decorative arts on the throne are very similar. Earlier in Nepal, it was customary to call the king an avatar (incarnation) of Vishnu and it was forbidden to worship Vishnu in Budhanilkanth.

And Pharaoh said, "Who is the Lord, that I should obey His voice to let Israel go? I do not know the Lord, nor will I let Israel go" (Exodus 5:2). The people of Nepal worship the king as god (dev). Thus, we see Prithvi Narayan Shah Dev, Mahendra Shah Dev, Birendra Shah Dev, Gyanendra Shah Dev.

Shah is an Islamic surname that comes from Iran and Dev means the title of god. In Nepal, Shah Dynasty rules started as Jethro did in Israel.

15And Moses said to his father-in-law, "Because the people come to me to inquire of God. 16 When they have a difficulty, they come to me, and I judge between one and another; and I make known the statutes of God and His laws."17 So Moses' father-in-law said to him, "The thing that you do is not good. 18Both you and these people who are with you will surely wear yourselves out. For this thing is too much for you; you are not able to perform it by yourself. 19 Listen now to my voice; I will give you counsel, and God will be with you: Stand before God for the people, so that you may bring the difficulties to God. 20And you shall teach them the statutes and the laws, and show them the way in which they must walk and the work they must do. 21 Moreover you shall select from all the people able men, such as fear God, men of truth, hating covetousness; and place such over them to be rulers of thousands, rulers of hundreds, rulers of fifties, and rulers of tens. 22 And let them judge the people at all times. Then it will be that every great matter they shall bring to you, but every small matter they themselves shall judge. So it will be easier for you, for they will bear the burden with you. 23 If you do this thing, and God so commands you, then you will be able to endure, and all this people will also go to their place in peace."24 So Moses heeded the voice of his father-in-law and did all that he had said. 25 And Moses chose able men out of all Israel, and made them heads over the people: rulers of thousands, rulers of hundreds, rulers of fifties, and rulers of tens. 26 So they judged the people at all times; the hard cases they brought to Moses, but they judged every small case themselves.[27] *Then Moses let his father-in-law depart, and he went his way to his own land. (Exodus 18:15-27)*

Perhaps, the Nepali people have little knowledge about this matter because the rules and regulations for filling mixed flower baskets have also been reduced. But it is focused on the biblical basis. Regarding the two types of Aryans, it can be assumed that the surname of the rulers of Iran was Shah and the background of the Shah dynasty of Nepal was Iranian. There is a snake on the crown of the King of Egypt and the crown of Nepal.

It can be assumed that the hexagon sign is the first in Nepal. Did the Dalits come together? But in any case, the swastika sign is a sign of the Aryan race. The Germans under the dictator Hitler killed the Jews. No matter how it manifests, it is an oppressive sign of oppressing other communities and building only their own state.

CHAPTER **7**

Political Foundation

BEGINNING AND FOUNDATION

And Jethro, the priest of Midian, Moses' father-in-law, heard of all that God had done for Moses and for Israel His people—that the Lord had brought Israel out of Egypt. [2] Then Jethro, Moses' father-in-law, took Zipporah, Moses' wife, after he had sent her back, [3] with her two sons, of whom the name of one was Gershom (for he said, "I have been a stranger in a foreign land") [4] and the name of the other was Eliezer (for he said, "The God of my father was my help, and delivered me from the sword of Pharaoh"); [5] and Jethro, Moses' father-in-law, came with his sons and his wife to Moses in the wilderness, where he was encamped at the mountain of God. [6] Now he had said to Moses, "I, your father-in-law Jethro, am coming to you with your wife and her two sons with her." [7] So Moses went out to meet his father-in law, bowed down, and kissed him. And they asked each other about their well-being, and they went into the tent. [8] And Moses told his father-in-law all that the Lord had done to Pharaoh and to the Egyptians for Israel's sake, all the hardship that had come upon them on the way, and how the Lord had delivered them. [9] Then Jethro rejoiced for all the good which the Lord had done for Israel, whom He had delivered out of the hand of the Egyptians. [10] And Jethro said, "Blessed be the Lord, who has delivered you out of the hand of the Egyptians and out of the hand of Pharaoh, and who has delivered the people from under the hand of the Egyptians. [11] Now I know that the Lord is greater than all the gods; for in the very thing in which they behaved proudly, He was above them." [12] Then Jethro, Moses' father-in-law, took a burnt offering and other sacrifices to offer to God. And Aaron came with all the elders of Israel to eat bread with Moses' father-in-law before God.[13] And so it was, on the next day, that Moses sat to judge the people, and the people stood before Moses from morning until evening. [14] So when Moses' father-in-law saw all that he did for the people, he said, "What is this thing that you are doing for the people? Why do you alone sit, and all the people stand before you from morning until evening?"[15] And Moses said to his father-in-law, "Because the people come to me to inquire of God. [16] When they have a difficulty, they come to me, and I judge between one and another; and I make known the statutes of God and His laws."[17] So Moses' father-in-law said to him, "The thing that you do is not good. [18]Both you and these people who are with you will surely wear yourselves out. For this thing is too much for you; you are not able to perform it by yourself. [19] Listen now to my voice; I will give you counsel, and God will be with you: Stand before God for the people, so that you may bring the difficulties to God. [20]And you shall teach them the statutes and the laws, and show them the way in which they must walk and the work they must do. [21] Moreover you shall select from all the people able men, such as fear God, men of truth, hating covetousness; and place such over them to be rulers of thousands, rulers of hundreds, rulers of fifties, and rulers of tens. [22] And let them judge the people at all times. Then it will be that every great matter they shall bring to you, but every small matter they themselves shall judge. So it will be easier for you, for they will bear the burden with you. [23] If you do this thing, and God so commands you, then you will be able to endure, and all this people will also go to their place in peace."[24] So Moses heeded the voice of his father-in-law and did all that he had said. [25] And Moses chose able men out of all Israel, and made them heads over the people: rulers of thousands, rulers of hundreds, rulers of fifties, and rulers of tens. [26] So they judged the people at all times; the hard cases they brought to Moses, but they judged every small case themselves.[27] Then Moses let his father-in-law depart, and he went his way to his own land. (Exodus 18:1-27)

In almost all countries laws have been made on the basis of this passage.

The beginning of language

Mongols used to greet each other in their own language. Gurung, Magar, Rai, Limbu, and others all have their own greetings. **Meaning of shalom**

In the untouchable community, it was common practice to salute. It comes from the Hebrew word shalom. Shalom used to be called Salam (salute). There is also a custom of saying *Salamlekhum* in the Islamic language. Especially because it comes from Hebrew.

The Hebrew word for the sign of peace in the Old Testament

The meaning of Shalom used to be broader than it is now. At that time, this word was known to mean completeness, wholeness, welfare (meaning good health), wealth, beauty, security and harmony. Addressing any person with the word shalom means saying, "How are you?" In addition to asking about his well-being, it is also understood that he expressed that welfare intention to him.

In the Greek language, the word Shalom is used in parallel. *Important Names of God* (Chhatra Subba Paul, p. 257).

When meeting people from other communities, earlier Dalit community used to greet them as Shalom, but now, this word is not so popular. Now almost everyone says Namaste or Namaskar.

Divisions and Races of the Ancient World

From Bible Journey (Balakumari, pp. 162-163)

In Nepal, you can hear it called "Shyambarna." Shyam means white. My guess is that probably it came from the descendants of Shem (Shambarna or Shembarna). Perhaps, they were the first generation of the Kirants because the Shyambarna people often look whitish. But when I researched the language below, (Descendants of Japheth) I found this (p.163):

Gomer

1. Magog

2. Madai

3. Javan

4. Tubal

5. Meshech

6. Tiras

Madai's children's language Turkish are also spoken in Turkish Kurdistan and other countries.

These Medians are found in few places in various verses of the Bible.

Now it came to pass in the days of Ahasuerus (this was the Ahasuerus who reigned over one hundred and twenty-seven provinces, from India to Ethiopia), [2] in those days when King Ahasuerus sat on the throne of his kingdom, which was in Shushanthe citadel, [3] that in the third year of his reign he made a feast for all his officials and servants—the powers of Persia and Media, the nobles, and the princes of the provinces being before him. (Esther 1:1-3)

At that time, Asia was very large. Those closest to him being Carshena, Shethar, Admatha, Tarshish, Meres, Marsena, and Memucan, the seven princes of Persia and Media, who had access to the king's presence, and who ranked highest in the kingdom. (Esther 1:14)

The New Testament believer is also seen at the time of Pentecost.

Now, when He had spoken these things, while they watched, He was taken up, and a cloud received Him out of their sight. And while they looked steadfastly toward heaven as He went up, behold, two men stood by them in white apparel. (Acts 1:9-10)

Medes were among the people of 12 countries. These Medes and the way Nepali tailor communities live, tolerate, eat and drink, observe hospitality, respect, and want peace, do not interfere with others, live a simple life and ask for money by playing five musical instruments in marriages are similar.

This Medes community does not like to mix with other communities. Their ancestors are Aramasichs. At various times, they came to Syria to seek refuge due to conflict and fighting in their country, and the Syrian government also gave shelter to these refugees. However, they were forced to adopt the name of Islam and were forbidden to speak their original language. In the same community, the person who sews clothes is pronounced Terti but the one who calls him is tailor.

Source-Veterinarian Farhan Mohamad

I have taken all these sources myself sitting with him and his family. You shall not muzzle an ox while it treads out the grain. (Deuteronomy 25:4)

THE CUSTOM OF LEVIRATE MARRIAGE

"If brothers dwell together, and one of them dies and has no son, the widow of the dead man shall not be married to a stranger outside the family; her husband's brother shall go in to her, take her as his wife, and perform the duty of a husband's brother to her. And it shall be that the firstborn son which she bears will succeed to the name of his dead brother, that his name may not be blotted out of Israel. (Deuteronomy 25:5-6)

It is found in different places of Nepal especially in Rai, Limbu, Sherpa, Magar, Gurung, Tamang communities.

CELEBRATING BIRTHDAYS

Now it came to pass on the third day, which was Pharaoh's birthday, that he made a feast for all his servants; and he lifted up the head of the chief butler and of the chief baker among his servants. (Genesis 40:20)

But when Herod's birthday was celebrated, the daughter of Herodias danced before them and pleased Herod. (Matthew 14:6)

The tradition of celebrating birthdays is not Nepali but biblical.

THE PRACTICE OF WEARING CHARMS IS BIBLICAL

The practice of wearing a charm as a protection against any mischief or evil was a common thing in the ancient Near Eastern countries. Charms are often made of jewelled gems, stones, shells, beads, metal, or other belonging. And sometimes, prayers or mantras were used in these charms.

[18] In that day the Lord will take away the finery: the jingling anklets, the scarves, and the crescents; [19] the pendants, the bracelets, and the veils;[20] the headdresses, the leg ornaments, and the headbands;the perfume boxes, the charms,[21] and the rings; the nose jewels,[22] the festal apparel, and the mantles;The outer garments, the purses,[23] and the mirrors;the fine linen, the turbans, and the robes. (Isaiah 3:18-23)

Jews are very straightforward and honest.

1. All the countries around us are moving ahead in terms of development, but among them, China is preparing itself to be number one in the world. The India of the Brahmins is getting weaker and weaker. But with the collusion (participation) of Westerners and Brahmins, such true news is not allowed to be propagated outside the media.

2. Aryan Brahmins who have ruled India also admit that they are from the Middle East like the Jews. From this, it can be understood that Jews and Aryan Brahmins do not have their own home.

3. Jews in India have been ranked in NGO infiltration of various non-governmental organizations. In this way, the honest Jews have been misled.

Arya Brahmins of this type seem to be dangerous enemies of the world. They talk about non-violence by being thankful, but they don't allow us to confront them openly like Palestine. These same people killed Gandhi and considered themselves to be the biggest Gandhian in the world.

The difference between the world's two famous anti-human enemies is that Zionists have always maintained their identity.

Looking at the history, no matter how many attacks were made on them, they loved their religion and culture. (From the dictionary verse 712)

New Testament Commentary taken from John 4

Leviticus 7:1 Priests who eat tails (mentioned three times)

Then, he took the fat and the fat tail, all the fat that was on the entrails, the fatty lobe attached to the liver, the two kidneys and their fat, and the right thigh. (Leviticus 8:25)

And the fat from the bull and the ram—the fatty tail, what covers the entrails and the kidneys, and the fatty lobe attached to the liver. (Leviticus 9:19)

Exodus 20: Page 144 from Old Testament Commentary

Do not worship idols

Do not touch the dead (Leviticus 21:1)

[7]Then, the eyes of both of them were opened, and they knew that they were naked; and they sewed fig leaves together and made themselves coverings.[8] And they heard the sound of the Lord God walking in the garden in the cool of the day, and Adam and his wife hid themselves from the presence of the Lord God among the trees of the garden. (Genesis 3:7-8)

LEATHER CLOTHING

Also, for Adam and his wife, the Lord God made tunics of skin, and clothed them. (Genesis 3:21)

TRUMPET

And the Lord spoke to Moses, saying: ² "Make two silver trumpets for yourself; you shall make them of hammered work; you shall use them for calling the congregation and for directing the movement of the camps. ³ When they blow both of them, all the congregation shall gather before you at the door of the tabernacle of meeting. ⁴ But if they blow only one, then the leaders, the heads of the divisions of Israel, shall gather to you. ⁵ When you sound the advance, the camps that lie on the east side shall then begin their journey. ⁶ When you sound the advance the second time, then the camps that lie on the south side shall begin their journey; they shall sound the call for them to begin their journeys. ⁷ And when the assembly is to be gathered together, you shall blow, but not sound the advance. ⁸ The sons of Aaron, the priests, shall blow the trumpets; and these shall be to you as an ordinance forever throughout your generations. ⁹ "When you go to war in your land against the enemy who oppresses you, then you shall sound an alarm with the trumpets, and you will be remembered before the Lord your God, and you will be saved from your enemies. ¹⁰ Also in the day of your gladness, in your appointed feasts, and at the beginning of your months, you shall blow the trumpets over your burnt offerings and over the sacrifices of your peace offerings; and they shall be a memorial for you before your God: I am the Lord your God." (Numbers 10:1-10)

ABOUT THE BLACKSMITH

"Behold, I have created the blacksmith who blows the coals in the fire, who brings forth an instrument for his work; and I have created the spoiler to destroy. (Isaiah 54:16)

I have created the blacksmith.

In Exodus chapter 31, God chose Bezalel and made him full of skills and abilities and appointed Oholiab to help Bezalel. (Also study Exodus 35.)

What happened after people sinned? They became naked and the relationship broke. The reference of craftsman began from here. Later, in the exodus, various tasks have been distributed or God has given various skills and gifts. It is written there that the gift will last forever. Noah's sons are scattered everywhere and have reached Lhasa. They became known as Mongolians.

Most Nepalese say that they are independent and self-respecting people. Of course, we have many reasons to be proud. For example, Mount Everest is ours, Gautama Buddha was born in our country, who is known as the messenger of Peace. The brave Gorkhali who defeated the British with khukuri or saved the country from slavery are the heroes of our country. Similarly, there are many other minerals that we should be proud of.

Some people say that India has developed because of colonization by the British. While some say that our country is fine, it has not been oppressed by anyone yet, but some say that if the British had colonized for a few years, we would have developed like other countries. This is how we live remembering the past. We have talked about the country, but now, we will take some time to pay some attention to our personal, social, and religious aspects.

Prithvi Narayan Shah united Nepal as a flower garden of four castes and thirty-six varnas. But what are these four castes? Where did it come from? How did it come to be? Why is there such a big wall of untouchability within these four castes? Why so much struggle?

Different people made history by trying in different ways. The community tried to get the identity, but the internal injuries, wounds, and bruises could not be treated.

ABOUT HEALING FROM WOUNDS AND INJURIES

Wounds or injuries, especially tripping on any part of the body, cutting firewood, or cutting hands while cutting grass, can be treated in an easy way. Now, before treatment of any illness like headache, vomiting, many questions are asked.

I remember when I was a child. My mother had studied some Ayurvedic medicine. Baba used to bring various herbs from the forest, mountains and fields, dried them, cooked them, crushed them, sorted them, and prepared substances with mixed ingredients. If someone had a pimple or a sore throat and suffered from a disease, then only after holding the pimple or sore throat and checking it, reddening the blade of a beard cutter in a fire pit, and then putting it again in water and cleaning it, the pimple operation was done. The same kind of medicine would be given to a person who had eaten or suffered from poison. If someone came sick with an injury, he would treat them and send them away. But if someone mentally ill came, they used to take a lot of time and interrogate them, but at that time, I was a child. So, I didn't care that much. Sometimes, when a woman came with a sick child, the mother would ask for the history before giving the medicine. I used to ask like this, "daughter/child, what happened? Since when did this happen? How did it happen? How many days has it been? Is this child sick?" He would keep asking until he found out how it all started. He would give Ayurvedic medicine only after finding out.

I used to get upset seeing that child crying and would tell my mother. The mother made this child cry and everyone in the house was sad, he couldn't sleep, and he couldn't eat. Make the medicine you asked for and send it to me. So that we can eat, live and sleep in peace. But the mother used to reply like this, "My son, listen to me. Any disease starts at a certain point, from a cause. Why did you get sick? When did it happen? How did it happen? Medicines will not work until all these are discovered." I vividly remember saying that the disease must be diagnosed before the treatment. At that time, I did not like that mother's words and used to laugh at it as a joke.

But now, if a medical doctor goes to any place for some reason, the doctors ask the same way as the mother used to ask at that time.

And medicine is given only after the disease is detected, and surely, we have got rid of more and more diseases.

Now comes the disease that has been bothering us for years among the four communities living in our beautiful country. It is the biggest ethnic disease among us. It should not be torn apart and the pus removed or thrown away.

WHO FIRST CAME TO NEPAL OR WHO IS THE ABORIGINE (INDEGENOUS RESIDENT)?

Certainly, Brahma created five types of people in India and Nepal. Perhaps, it may be a lot of fantasy, but the evidence given by the real statement and history seems to show that our ethnic conflict is riper than curing the disease. And the people of almost four communities of Nepal are in various pains (injury or illness) and it has reached a situation where they cannot get up.

Before we find the disease at once, we will go into the origin of man and try to understand how different communities entered Nepal at different times through migration.

1. ADAM TAILOR

After God created man, he fell into sin. After the fall, we realized that we were naked. After that, Adam tied fig leaves together and made his wife a *chaubandi choli* (a small blouse) and sari. And Eve made her husband Adam a trouser. At that time, sewing machines were not yet made. No time has been given as to how many days it took to sew and cover the nakedness by hand. A long time ago, in our country Nepal, our ancestors used to make clothes by making cotton and khadi from silk and ivory, as well as various plants. The person who sews the same clothes is named Tailor.

And they heard the sound of the Lord God walking in the garden in the cool of the day, and Adam and his wife hid themselves from the presence of the Lord God among the trees of the garden. (Genesis 3:8)

Now a certain woman named Lydia heard us. She was a seller of purple from the city of Thyatira, who worshiped God. The Lord opened her heart to heed the things spoken by Paul. (Acts 16:14) (Lydia Tailor)

If we Christians understand the Bible properly, the name of the first person of creation or our father is Adam tailor and mother's name is Eve Damini. We are all their children. If profession is to be made a caste, then this post should be removed or we should accept that tailor is the father of all of us.

Another thing happened in our society. Leather workers are called *Sarki.*

Let's look at Genesis 3:21 from the Bible, "Also for Adam and his wife the Lord God made tunics of skin, and clothed them."

God is a tanner. The Lord God made or sewed skin clothes for Adam and his wife. In our society, leather workers are called untouchables. Now, our God and His sons and daughters become Sarki. The sons and daughters of the God who sews leather jackets and make leather clothes are Sarki.

Nicodemus said to Him, "How can a man be born when he is old? Can he enter a second time into his mother's womb and be born?" (John 3:4)

John also sewed a camel jacket and wore it. He also sewed the waist belt himself. Was John also Sarki?

He is lodging with Simon, a tanner, whose house is by the sea. He will tell you what you must do. (Acts 10:6)

Send therefore to Joppa and call Simon here, whose surname is Peter. He is lodging in the house of Simon, a tanner, by the sea. When he comes, he will speak to you. (Acts10:32)

(The tanner was in the house of Simon.)

After these things, Paul departed from Athens and went to Corinth. [2] And he found a certain Jew named Aquila, born in Pontus, who had recently come from Italy with his wife Priscilla (because Claudius had commanded all the Jews to depart from Rome); and he came to them. [3] So, because he was of the same trade, he stayed with them and worked; for by occupation, they were tentmakers. (Acts 18:1-3)

Both Paul and Simon were Jewish tanners. Both of them had the same profession of making leather tents.

HOW WAS THE BIBLE WRITTEN?

1. Papyrus made from the outer part of the tree fount in Egypt and Syria. The word of the Bible was written on it. That's why we get the word Bible from Byblos.

2. By removing skins from sheep, goats, and deer

3. Vellum was prepared by removing the skin from the cow's calf and the word was written on it with red ink.

4. A clay mold was made and the word was written on the clay by the potter.

5. Then, a lot of paper was made and mixed and made thick and kept in a long roll from 6 to 44 meters.

While we were looking at the leather above, God himself was a tanner. If the tanner did not write the Bible on the skin, we would not have the chance today to read the Bible and know God. God is our creator tanner and your sons and daughters are all tanners.

THE GIFT OF ENGINEERING

We learn from here about the gift of craftsman in Genesis when Noah built the ark. Of course, more and more metal was used in making that ship. For example, it seems impossible to make a ship by melting iron in a fiery furnace without the skill of God. Building a wooden ship is impossible without the help of iron. Therefore, there is nothing more difficult than being a craftsman first.

Make yourself an ark of gopher wood; make rooms in the ark, and cover it inside and outside with pitch. (Genesis 6:14)

These three were the sons of Noah, and from these, the whole earth was populated. (Genesis 9:19)

2 The sons of Japheth were Gomer, Magog, Madai, Javan, Tubal, Meshech, and Tiras. 3 The sons of Gomer were Ashkenaz, Riphath, and Togarmah. 4 The sons of Javan were Elishah, Tarshish, Kittim, and Dodanim. 5 From these, the coastland peoples of the Gentiles were separated into their lands, everyone according to his language, according to their families, into their nations. (Genesis 10:2-5)

These verses describe the children of Japheth. They went to the north to settle in the territory of the Black Sea and the Caspian Sea. They later became the ancestors of the Medes, Greeks, and the Indo-European white people of Europe and Asia. In the next book I will give a brief description of Medes.

BEZALEL AND OHOLIAB

30 And Moses said to the children of Israel, "See, the Lord has called by name Bezalel the son of Uri, the son of Hur, of the tribe of Judah; 31 and He has filled him with the Spirit of God, in wisdom and understanding, in knowledge and all manner of workmanship, 32 to design artistic works, to work in gold and silver and bronze, 33 in cutting jewels for setting, in carving wood, and to work in all manner of artistic workmanship.34 "And He has put in his heart the ability to teach, in him and Aholiab the son of Ahisamach, of the tribe of Dan. 35 He has filled them with skill to do all manner of work of the engraver and the designer and the tapestry maker, in blue, purple, and scarlet thread, and fine linen, and of the weaver— those who do every work and those who design artistic works. (Exodus 35:30-35)

In our society, the gift given by God to the tailors, tanners and siyojikars, who have been gifted with skills, and talents for years, is still seen in the customs and professions. If you look at the music field, it is mostly from the tailor community.

Looking at the old Nepali word language, no one questions how tailor came to be.

Arrival of aboriginals

It is assumed that they entered Nepal riding a Mongolian horse with flat nose and small eyes. But it is also reasonable to question how Mongolians entered Mongolia.

BENEI MANASHE

Then the children of Israel did evil in the sight of the Lord. So, the Lord delivered them into the hand of Midian for seven years, [2] and the hand of Midian prevailed against Israel. Because of the Midianites, the children of Israel made for themselves the dens, the caves, and the strongholds which are in the mountains. [3] So it was, whenever Israel had sown, Midianites would come up; also Amalekites and the people of the East would come up against them. [4] Then they would encamp against them and destroy the produce of the earth as far as Gaza, and leave no sustenance for Israel, neither sheep nor ox nor donkey. [5] For they would come up with their livestock and their tents, coming in as numerous as locusts; both they and their camels were without number; and they would enter the land to destroy it. [6] So, Israel was greatly impoverished because of the Midianites, and the children of Israel cried out to the Lord. [7] And it came to pass, when the children of Israel cried out to the Lord because of the Midianites, [8] that the Lord sent a prophet to the children of Israel, who said to them, "Thus says the Lord God of Israel: 'I brought you up from Egypt and brought you out of the house of bondage; [9] and I delivered you out of the hand of the Egyptians and out of the hand of all who oppressed you, and drove them out before you and gave you their land. [10] Also I said to you, "I am the Lord your God; do not fear the gods of the Amorites, in whose land you dwell." But you have not obeyed My voice.'" [11] Now the Angel of the Lord came and sat under the terebinth tree which was in Ophrah, which belonged to Joash the Abiezrite, while his son Gideon threshed wheat in the winepress, in order to hide it from the Midianites. [12] And the Angel of the Lord appeared to him, and said to him, "The Lord is with you, you mighty man of valor!"[13] Gideon said to Him, "O my lord, if the Lord is with us, why then has all this happened to us? And where are all His miracles which our fathers told us about, saying, 'Did not the Lord bring us up from Egypt?' But now, the Lord has forsaken us and delivered us into the hands of the Midianites."[14] Then, the Lord turned to him and said, "Go in this might of yours, and you shall save Israel from the hand of the Midianites. Have I not sent you?"[15] So he said to Him, "O my Lord, how can I save Israel? Indeed my clan is the weakest in Manasseh, and I am the least in my father's house." (Judges 6:1-15)

Today, the faces of the children of Manasseh are present in aboriginal Gurung, Rai, Tamang, Limbu, Magar society, from eating and drinking to various activities. Of course, it will. But the children of the same Manasseh are found in Nepal, Bangladesh, India, Manipur, Mizoram, Myanmar, Afghanistan, Arab and other countries of the world. Some people in Europe, Russia and Africa have now gone to their own private country, Israel. But what I mean is to give the background of our residents and it is based on the Bible. Various histories and evidences tell us that our residents first entered. We are told about the Licchhavi period in various ways and we have also read them at different times.

When Prithvi Narayan Shah united Nepal, our Gurungs, Rais, Limbus, Magars, and Tamangs would not have fought naked. I mean they were not naked. At that time, of course, Siojikar sewed clothes and was responsible for playing instruments in various auspicious functions.

There were also tanners. They were also responsible for making various leather shoes, making belts, making tents, and turning the instruments with leather to be played during auspicious activities and at different times and making khari on the madal. At that time, there was no discrimination between the Mongolian communities, Silpkar, Charamkar, Siojikar community, but how did it start? The struggle started only after the entry of Aryans. (Pundit Madhav Upadhyaya)

Regarding whether the Newar community is Aryan or Mongolian, it can be assumed that they were Mongolian at first but were mixed after the arrival of Aryans.

Compared to other communities, the Newar community has faced complex problems due to internal discrimination and it seems that it will continue to happen. This is because pastors of the Newari community preach about caste from the pulpit, not by everyone, but especially by those who have attained higher education from outside and inside.

CHAPTER 8

Indian Brahmins and Struggle Among Jew Dalits

THE BRAHMINS AND THE JEWS

Not long ago, the American media focused on the plight of the oppressed Harijan community in India.

V.T. Rajeshekar is a famous Dalit journalist of India. He is the editor of *Dalit Voice*. According to *Human Rights Watch,* Rajeshekar is a target of the Indian police and the Indian government. Rajeshekar himself did not belong to the Dalit community; he belonged to a backward caste—Bunt community.

"Old memories. New Histories (RE) Discovering the Past of Jews Dalits" – this paper studies the process of self-identification and historical memory formation of the Benei Ephraim in Andhra Pradesh. "The Bene Ephraim" community who are untouchables, have been following Judaism before 1990.

Key Words: Judaism, India, History, Dalits: Introduction: 30/40 years ago, where we are still living. Grandmother said that one day, we would go back to Israel.

There was an old woman who had been living in India for centuries. Maybe, this old woman was also told by her grandparents.

Or they may have been given oral education. Our ancestors have been living as slaves here in India for many years and have become

Dalits. There will come a person like Moses. He will come to India and we will be worshiped by these priests of Baal deity who will build temples everywhere and worship the art of hand. We are being tortured physically and mentally.

One day, we will be freed from all these tortures and freed from slavery. We will definitely go to our promised land, Israel, in our time. Are we going to change the thinking of our Nepalese untouchables or Harijans who have been living in our Nepal like that old Dalit Jewish woman? Where did we come from? How did we come? Is it time to consider why we are different from the worshipers of these handicrafts?

In India, the practice of calling Adi and aboriginal Dalits or Untouchables is understood to have occurred only after the arrival of the priest of the Baal deity. Even in Nepal, the sons and daughters of Benei Manasseh or their descendants, who geographically have Mongolian faces with small eyes and pointed noses, identify that there were twenty-two and twenty-four kingdoms. They did not worship handicrafts. They used to worship ancestors or dead fathers and mothers. At that time, the descendants of Benei Ephraim who were in India are now called untouchables.

• Both of these communities lived together. Looking at the history, Vishwakarma community earned their livelihood by making weapons and tools.

• Tanner community provided various types of leather shoes, waist belts, khukuri, and different types of leather. Most of these communities have the surname Mirza. The surname Mirza comes from a place called Armenia. There was a prince named Mirza. Reading the history of Chamars in India also proves that their Chamar kingdom existed at one time.

The tailor community is not only common in Nepal, but this surname is called the profession of cloth or sewing clothes. This surname also started from Turkey. It is called Darzi in Turkish Kurdistan. In Israel, it is called *Talmuol*. It started especially from Israel.

These materials and sources prove that we are descendants of Benei Ephraim.

Now, the tailoring community plays instruments. Why and how do the priests who carry the ark in the auspicious work and the similarity of Nepal's Panche Baja (five instruments) fit well?

Another evidence of priests' eating tails is in the Bible. If we cannot see the similarity between the two, then we ourselves are to blame.

All these pieces of evidence prove that:

- The Mongols are the descendants of Benei Manaseh.

- The so-called Untouchable communities are the priestly descendants of Levi.

- The Shah dynasties are the descendants of Pharoah.

- The Aryans are the worshippers of the deity called Baal. The one and the same God created all humankind, whom we address as the Lord God.

Therefore, since we are children of one Father our Creator God, we need to stop quarrelling among ourselves and oppressing one another, and we should learn to live in peace.

BRAHMA

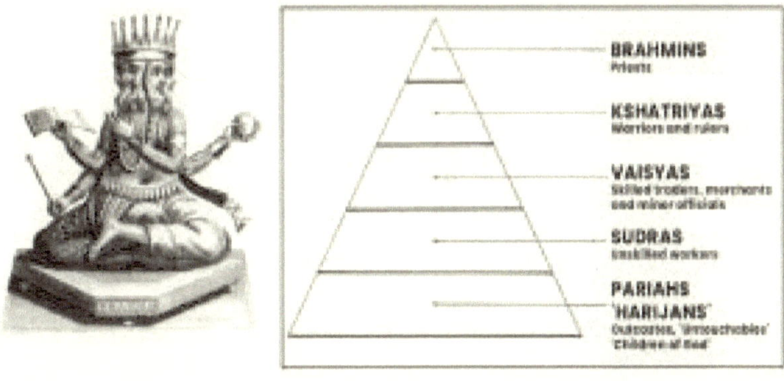

Meaning the Creator

Photo Courtesy: BBC, "What is India's caste system?"

https://www.bbc.com/news/world-asia-india-35650616

CHAPTER 9

Jewish Lifestyle in Nepal

1. **Saturday as Sabbath day or holy day:** And the Lord spoke to Moses, saying, [2] "Speak to the children of Israel, and say to them: 'The feasts of the Lord, which you shall proclaim to be holy convocations, these are My feasts.' [3] 'Six days shall work be done, but the seventh day is a Sabbath of solemn rest, a holy convocation. You shall do no work on it; it is the Sabbath of the Lord in all your dwellings.' (Leviticus 23:1-3)

2. **Sacrifice of Atonement:** Dashain is the day of slaughter once in year or ten-day festival.

3. **Sankranti:** You shall offer up a cake of the first of your ground meal as a heave offering. (Numbers 15:20). Maghe Sakranti in Nepal and Thanksgiving Day in India are celebrated as a cake (*phulaura*) eating day.

4. **Charm:** Charm is mentioned in Nepali Dictionary page no. 229.

5. **Beginning of Political Leaders:** And the Lord spoke to Moses, saying, [2] "Make two silver trumpets for yourself; you shall make them of hammered work; you shall use them for calling the congregation and for directing the movement of the camps." (Numbers 10:1-2)

6. **The custom of releasing the bull:** It has been explained above.

7. **Blood in the bowl:** And Moses took half the blood and put it in basins, and half the blood he sprinkled on the altar (Exodus 24:6). Tika is to be put on after sprinkling the blood of sacrifice. Therefore, not even the first covenant was dedicated without blood (Hebrews 9:18).

8. **To give part or share:** (Dictionary 126): In various parts of Nepal, Radi, wool, lamb is given to the children of Levi or to the worshiper's family at a wedding or in some sacred function.

9. **Priests who eat tails:** In Nepal, the tails of sacrificed animals are the right of the tailor community and others cannot eat them.

Then, he took the fat and the fat tail, all the fat that was on the entrails, the fatty lobe attached to the liver, the two kidneys and their fat, and the right thigh (Leviticus 8:25). He also killed the bull and the ram as sacrifices of peace offerings, which were for the people. And Aaron's sons presented to him the blood, which he sprinkled all around on the altar, and the fat from the bull and the ram—the fatty tail, what covers the entrails and the kidneys, and the fatty lobe attached to the liver (Leviticus 9:18-19).

No one asks or questions how this custom came to Nepal, but they call it a community that eats tails as our tradition. The custom of eating or giving the tail has been clarified in the Bible's passages. To call it a tail-eating community is to lose its authority because God reserved the authority of the priesthood to the sons of Levi and it is not a man-made custom. Rather than this community calling itself untouchable, it is proper to glorify Jesus by believing that we have come from the tribe of Levi, the son of God.

10. **Method of administering justice:** Jethro taught Moses how to do justice (Exodus 18:1-27). This custom is still effective.

11. **Releasing the scapegoat:** Then Aaron shall cast lots for the two goats: one lot for the Lord and the other lot for the scapegoat. (Leviticus 16:8)

12. **The image of the calf:** They made a calf in Horeb, and worshiped the moulded image. (Psalm 106:19)

13. **Worship of the golden calf:**

Now when the people saw that Moses delayed coming down from the mountain, the people gathered together to Aaron, and said to him, "Come, make us gods that shall go before us; for as for this Moses, the man who brought us up out of the land of Egypt, we do not know what has become of him." [2] And Aaron said to them, "Break off the golden earrings which are in the ears of your wives, your sons, and your daughters, and bring them to me." [3] So all the people broke off the golden earrings which were in their ears, and brought them to Aaron. [4] And he received the gold from their hand, and he fashioned it with an engraving tool, and made a moulded calf. Then they said, "This is your god, O Israel, that brought you out of the land of Egypt!" [5] So when Aaron saw it, he built an altar before it. And Aaron made a proclamation and said, "Tomorrow is a feast to the Lord." [6] Then they rose early on the next day, offered burnt offerings, and brought peace offerings; and the people sat down to eat and drink, and rose up to play. [7] And the Lord said to Moses, "Go, get down! For your people whom you brought out of the land of Egypt have corrupted themselves. [8] They have turned aside quickly out of the way which I commanded them. They have made themselves a moulded calf, and worshiped it and sacrificed to it, and said, 'This is your god, O Israel, that brought you out of the land of Egypt!' " [9] And the Lord said to Moses, "I have seen this people, and indeed it is a stiff-necked people! [10] Now therefore, let Me alone, that My wrath may burn hot against them and I may consume them. And I will make of you a great nation." [11] Then Moses pleaded with the Lord his God, and said: "Lord, why does Your wrath burn hot against Your people whom You have brought out of the land of Egypt with great power and with a mighty hand? [12] Why should the Egyptians speak, and say, 'He brought them out to harm them, to kill them in the mountains, and to consume them from the face of the earth?' Turn from Your fierce wrath, and relent from this harm to

Your people. ¹³ Remember Abraham, Isaac, and Israel, Your servants, to whom You swore by Your own self, and said to them, 'I will multiply your descendants as the stars of heaven; and all this land that I have spoken of I give to your descendants, and they shall inherit it forever.'" ¹⁴ So the Lord relented from the harm which He said He would do to His people. ¹⁵And Moses turned and went down from the mountain, and the two tablets of the Testimony were in his hand. The tablets were written on both sides; on the one side and on the other they were written. ¹⁶Now the tablets were the work of God, and the writing was the writing of God engraved on the tablets. ¹⁷ And when Joshua heard the noise of the people as they shouted, he said to Moses, "There is a noise of war in the camp." ¹⁸But he said: "It is not the noise of the shout of victory, nor the noise of the cry of defeat, but the sound of singing I hear." ¹⁹ So it was, as soon as he came near the camp, that he saw the calf and the dancing. So, Moses' anger became hot, and he cast the tablets out of his hands and broke them at the foot of the mountain. ²⁰ Then, he took the calf which they had made, burned it in the fire, and ground it to powder; and he scattered it on the water and made the children of Israel drink it. ²¹ And Moses said to Aaron, "What did this people do to you that you have brought so great a sin upon them?" ²² So Aaron said, "Do not let the anger of my lord become hot. You know the people, that they are set on evil. ²³ For they said to me, 'Make us gods that shall go before us; as for this Moses, the man who brought us out of the land of Egypt, we do not know what has become of him.' ²⁴ And I said to them, 'Whoever has any gold, let them break it off.' So, they gave it to me, and I cast it into the fire, and this calf came out." ²⁵ Now, when Moses saw that the people were unrestrained (for Aaron had not restrained them, to their shame among their enemies), ²⁶ then Moses stood in the entrance of the camp, and said, "Whoever is on the Lord's side—come to me!" And all the sons of Levi gathered themselves together to him. ²⁷And he said to them, "Thus says the Lord God of Israel: 'Let every man put his sword on his side, and go in and out from entrance to entrance throughout the camp, and let every man kill his brother, every man his companion, and every man his neighbour.'" ²⁸ So the sons of Levi did according to the word of Moses. And about three thousand men of the people fell that day. ²⁹ Then Moses said, "Consecrate yourselves today to the Lord, that He may bestow on you a blessing this day, for every man has opposed his son and his brother."³⁰Now it came to pass on the next day that Moses said to the people, "You have committed a great sin. So now I will go up to the Lord; perhaps I can make atonement for your sin."³¹ Then Moses returned to the Lord and said, "Oh, these people have committed a great sin, and have made for themselves a god of gold!³² Yet now, if You will forgive their sin—but if not, I pray, blot me out of Your book which You have written."³³ And the Lord said to Moses, "Whoever has sinned against Me, I will blot him out of My book.³⁴ Now therefore, go, lead the people to the place of which I have spoken to you. Behold, My Angel shall go before you. Nevertheless, in the day when I visit for punishment, I will visit punishment upon them for their sin."³⁵ So the Lord plagued the people because of what they did with the calf which Aaron made. (Exodus 32:1-35)

14. **Oxen:** And King Ahaz cut off the panels of the carts, and removed the lavers from them; and he took down the Sea from the bronze oxen that were under it, and put it on a pavement of stones. (2 Kings 16:17)

15. **About the Trident (Trishul):** Now the sons of Eli were corrupt; they did not know the Lord. (1 Samuel 2:12)

16. **Purana:** Also, day by day, from the first day until the last day, he read from the Book of the Law of God. And they kept the feast seven days; and on the eighth day there was a sacred assembly, according to the prescribed manner. (Nehemiah 8:18)

17. **First fruit or Nwagi in Nepal:**

²⁸ "It shall be, in regard to their inheritance, that I am their inheritance. You shall give them no possession in Israel, for I am their possession. ²⁹ They shall eat the grain offering, the sin offering, and the trespass offering; every dedicated thing in Israel shall be theirs. ³⁰ The best of all first fruits of any kind, and every sacrifice of any kind from all your sacrifices, shall be the priest's; also, you shall give to the priest the first of your ground meal, to cause a blessing to rest on your house. [31] The priests shall not eat anything, bird or beast, that died naturally or was torn by wild beasts. (Ezekiel 44:28-31)

And the Lord spoke to Moses (Leviticus 23:9). Honour the Lord with your possessions, and with the first fruits of all your increase. (Proverbs 3:9)

18. **Tattooing:** The word of God prohibits to make any mark on the body. Nowadays, many personalities are making tattoos and marks. Tattoo ink is made by mixing different materials from the ashes of dead people. In various countries, it is now advised not to wear tattoos. Because it is understood that various diseases are produced by it.

Instruments:

19. **Narsinga:** For You are the glory of their strength, and in Your favour our horn is exalted. (Psalm 89:17)

Also, I will set his hand over the sea, and his right hand over the rivers (Psalms 89:25). Nar means a man, or a male, lion means strength. (In Hebrew, it means showing power.)

20. **Old Nepali Bible:** Then they took an oath before the Lord with a loud voice, with shouting and trumpets and rams' horns (2 Chronicles 15:14). Narsinga is written in Old Nepali Bible. Narasinga is also mentioned in Nepali new revised version and Hindi Bible (2 Chronicles15:14)

Holy Bible Hindi_O_V_1066/93-94/ 15MPL (35gsm) ISBN 81- 221-1067-3 c. Bible Society of India

Although the modern word is trumpet after correcting the old words in various Bible verses, the correct word in Hindi and Nepali is *narsinga.*

21. The meaning of horn is power: A lion in English is a powerful king of the forest or a powerful animal in Nepali.

This narsinga instrument is usually played at any auspicious function or before the start of the sacred marriage ceremony. The sound of this instrument is very sharp and melodious among the other instruments that are played when the bridegroom goes up to the hill to give good news or when the bridegroom goes to pick up the bride at a wedding. This instrument is played by a man or a male, which is why it is called Narasinga and it is played only by tailor worshipers or this holy community. In different corners of Nepal before the festival, people go to the hills and play Narsinga from house to house.

22. Musicians in the temple playing instruments (people who play instruments):

[31] *Now these are the men whom David appointed over the service of song in the house of the Lord, after the ark came to rest.* [32] *They were ministering with music before the dwelling place of the tabernacle of meeting, until Solomon had built the house of the Lord in Jerusalem, and they served in their office according to their order.* [33]*And these are the ones who ministered with their sons: Of the sons of the Kohathites were Heman the singer, the son of Joel, the son of Samuel,* [34] *the son of Elkanah, the son of Jeroham, the son of Eliel, the son of Toah,* [35] *the son of Zuph, the son of Elkanah, the son of Mahath, the son of Amasai,* [36] *the son of Elkanah, the son of Joel, the son of Azariah, the son of Zephaniah,* [37] *the son of Tahath, the son of Assir, the son of Ebiasaph, the son of Korah,* [38] *the son of Izhar, the son of Kohath, the son of Levi, the son of Israel.* [39]*And his brother Asaph, who stood at his right hand, was Asaph the son of Berachiah, the son of Shimea,* [40] *the son of Michael, the son of Baaseiah, the son of Malchijah,* [41] *the son of Ethni, the son of Zerah, the son of Adaiah,* [42] *the son of Ethan, the son of Zimmah, the son of Shimei,* [43] *the son of Jahath, the son of Gershon, the son of Levi.*[44] *Their brethren, the sons of Merari, on the left hand, were Ethan the son of Kishi, the son of Abdi, the son of Malluch,* [45] *the*

*son of Hashabiah, the son of Amaziah, the son of Hilkiah, * [46] *the son of Amzi, the son of Bani, the son of Shamer,* [47] *the son of Mahli, the son of Mushi, the son of Merari, the son of Levi.* [48] *And their brethren, the Levites, were appointed to every kind of service of the tabernacle of the house of God.* [49] *But Aaron and his sons offered sacrifices on the altar of burnt offering and on the altar of incense, for all the work of the Most Holy Place, and to make atonement for Israel, according to all that Moses the servant of God had commanded.* [50] *Now, these are the sons of Aaron: Eleazar his son, Phinehas his son, Abishua his son,* [51] *Bukki his son, Uzzi his son, Zerahiah his son,* [52] *Meraioth his son, Amariah his son, Ahitub his son,* [53] *Zadok his son, and Ahimaaz his son.* [54] *Now these are their dwelling places throughout their settlements in their territory, for they were given by lot to the sons of Aaron, of the family of the Kohathites:* [55] *They gave them Hebron in the land of Judah, with its surrounding common-lands.* [56] *But the fields of the city and its villages they gave to Caleb the son of Jephunneh.* [57] *And to the sons of Aaron they gave one of the cities of refuge, Hebron; also Libnah with its common-lands, Jattir, Eshtemoa with its common-lands,* [58] *Hilen with its common-lands, Debir with its common-lands,* [59] *Ashan with its common-lands, and Beth Shemesh with its common-lands.* [60] *And from the tribe of Benjamin: Geba with its common-lands, Alemeth with its common-lands, and Anathoth with its common-lands. All their cities among their families were thirteen.* [61] *To the rest of the family of the tribe of the Kohathites they gave by lot ten cities from half the tribe of Manasseh.* [62] *And to the sons of Gershon, throughout their families, they gave thirteen cities from the tribe of Issachar, from the tribe of Asher, from the tribe of Naphtali, and from the tribe of Manasseh in Bashan.* [63] *To the sons of Merari, throughout their families, they gave twelve cities from the tribe of Reuben, from the tribe of Gad, and from the tribe of Zebulun.* [64] *So the children of Israel gave these cities with their common-lands to the Levites.* [65] *And they gave by lot from the tribe of the children of Judah, from the tribe of the children of Simeon, and from the tribe of the children of Benjamin these cities which are called by their names.* [66] *Now some of the families of the sons of Kohath* *were given cities as their territory from the tribe of Ephraim. ⁶⁷And they gave them one of the cities of refuge, Shechem with its common-lands, in the mountains of Ephraim, also Gezer with its common-lands, ⁶⁸ Jokmeam with its common lands, Beth Horon with its common-lands, ⁶⁹Aijalon with its common-lands, and Gath Rimmon with its common-lands. ⁷⁰ And from the half-tribe of Manasseh: Aner with its common-lands and Bileam with its common-lands, for the rest of the family of the sons of Kohath.⁷¹ From the family of the half-tribe of Manasseh the sons of Gershon were given Golan in Bashan with its common lands and Ashtaroth with its common-lands. ⁷²And from the tribe of Issachar: Kedesh with its common-lands, Daberath with its common-lands, ⁷³ Ramoth with its common-lands, and Anem with its common-lands. ⁷⁴ And from the tribe of Asher: Mashal with its common-lands, Abdon with its common-lands, ⁷⁵ Hukok with its common-lands, and Rehob with its common-lands. ⁷⁶And from the tribe of Naphtali: Kedesh in Galilee with its common lands, Hammon with its common-lands, and Kirjathaim with its common-lands.⁷⁷From the tribe of Zebulun the rest of the children of Merari were given Rimmon with its common-lands and Tabor with its common-lands. ⁷⁸ And on the other side of the Jordan, across from Jericho, on the east side of the Jordan, they were given from the tribe of Reuben: Bezer in the wilderness with its common-lands, Jahzah with its common-lands, ⁷⁹Kedemoth with its common-lands, and Mephaath with its common-lands. ⁸⁰ And from the tribe of Gad: Ramoth in Gilead with its common-lands, Mahanaim with its common-lands. (1 Chronicles 6:31-80)*

23. **Traditions of Purana:** Also, day by day, from the first day until the last day, he read from the Book of the Law of God. And they kept the feast seven days; and on the eighth day, there was a sacred assembly, according to the prescribed manner. (Nehemiah 8:18)

24. **Name was giver according to profession:** Meonothai was the father of Ophrah. Seraiah was the father of Joab, the father of Ge Harashim. It was called this because its people were skilled workers. (1 Chronicles 4:14)

25. A bronze bull: And King Ahaz cut off the panels of the carts, and removed the lavers from them, and he took down the Sea from the bronze oxen that were under it, and put it on a pavement of stones. (2 Kings 16:17). At Pashupatinath or in most temples of Judah Surnames are kept according to the work of other gotras/clans.

Meonothai was the father of Ophrah. Seraiah was the father of Joab, the father of Ge Harashim. It was called this because its people were skilled workers. (1 Chronicles 4:14)

26. Dalits are forbidden to imitate: [14] Nevertheless they would not hear, but stiffened their necks, like the necks of their fathers, who did not believe in the Lord their God. [15]And they rejected His statutes and His covenant that He had made with their fathers, and His testimonies which He had testified against them; they followed idols, became idolaters, and went after the nations who were all around them, concerning whom the Lord had charged them that they should not do like them. (2 Kings 17:14-15)

Aryan society, without searching for its identity since centuries, saying that you are Harijans and not coming to worship the handicrafts made by you, trying to forcefully go or worshiping the handicrafts. It is understood that the Harijans or Dalit community violates human rights. In this sense, calling the true Lord Jesus as your Lord and Saviour in your heart means becoming a Christian by believing in Christ or considering your body as the temple of Christ.

27. Bread, roti, raisins:

So, they brought the ark of God, and set it in the midst of the tabernacle that David had erected for it. Then they offered burnt offerings and peace offerings before God. [2] And when David had finished offering the burnt offerings and the peace offerings, he blessed the people in the name of the Lord. [3] Then he distributed to everyone of Israel, both man and woman, to everyone a loaf of bread, a piece of meat, and a cake of raisins. [4] And he appointed some of the Levites to minister before the ark of the Lord, to commemorate, to thank, and to praise the Lord

God of Israel: ⁵ *Asaph the chief, and next to him Zechariah, then Jeiel, Shemiramoth, Jehiel, Mattithiah, Eliab, Benaiah, and Obed Edom: Jeiel with stringed instruments and harps, but Asaph made music with cymbals;* ⁶ *Benaiah and Jahaziel the priests regularly blew the trumpets before the ark of the covenant of God. (1 Chronicles 16:1-6)*

28. *Asthi* or bones relics:

Then Joseph fell on his father's face and wept over him, and kissed him. ²And Joseph commanded his servants the physicians to embalm his father. So, the physicians embalmed Israel. ³Forty days were required for him, for such are the days required for those who are embalmed; and the Egyptians mourned for him seventy days. ⁴ Now when the days of his mourning were past, Joseph spoke to the household of Pharaoh, saying, "If now I have found favour in your eyes, please speak in the hearing of Pharaoh, saying, ⁵ 'My father made me swear, saying, "Behold, I am dying; in my grave which I dug for myself in the land of Canaan, there you shall bury me." Now therefore, please let me go up and bury my father, and I will come back.'" ⁶ And Pharaoh said, "Go up and bury your father, as he made you swear." ⁷ So Joseph went up to bury his father; and with him went up all the servants of Pharaoh, the elders of his house, and all the elders of the land of Egypt, ⁸ as well as all the house of Joseph, his brothers, and his father's house. Only their little ones, their flocks, and their herds they left in the land of Goshen. ⁹And there went up with him both chariots and horsemen, and it was a very great gathering. ¹⁰ Then they came to the threshing floor of Atad, which is beyond the Jordan, and they mourned there with a great and very solemn lamentation. He observed seven days of mourning for his father. ¹¹ And when the inhabitants of the land, the Canaanites, saw the mourning at the threshing floor of Atad, they said, "This is a deep mourning of the Egyptians." Therefore, its name was called Abel Mizraim, which is beyond the Jordan. ¹² So his sons did for him just as he had commanded them. ¹³ For his sons carried him to the land of Canaan, and buried him in the cave of the field of Machpelah, before Mamre, which Abraham bought with the field from Ephron the

Hittite as property for a burial place. ¹⁴ And after he had buried his father, Joseph returned to Egypt, he and his brothers and all who went up with him to bury his father. ¹⁵ When Joseph's brothers saw that their father was dead, they said, "Perhaps Joseph will hate us, and may actually repay us for all the evil which we did to him." ¹⁶ So they sent messengers to Joseph, saying, "Before your father died he commanded, saying, ¹⁷ 'Thus you shall say to Joseph: "I beg you, please forgive the trespass of your brothers and their sin; for they did evil to you."' Now, please, forgive the trespass of the servants of the God of your father." And Joseph wept when they spoke to him. ¹⁸ Then his brothers also went and fell down before his face, and they said, "Behold, we are your servants." ¹⁹ Joseph said to them, "Do not be afraid, for am I in the place of God? ²⁰ But as for you, you meant evil against me; but God meant it for good, in order to bring it about as it is this day, to save many people alive. ²¹ Now therefore, do not be afraid; I will provide for you and your little ones." And he comforted them and spoke kindly to them. (Genesis 50:1-21)

By faith Joseph, when he was dying, made mention of the departure of the children of Israel, and gave instructions concerning his bones. (Hebrews 11:22)

And Moses took the bones of Joseph with him, for he had placed the children of Israel under solemn oath, saying, "God will surely visit you, and you shall carry up my bones from here with you." (Exodus 13:19)

The bones of Joseph, which the children of Israel had brought up out of Egypt, they buried at Shechem, in the plot of ground which Jacob had bought from the sons of Hamor the father of Shechem for one hundred pieces of silver, and which had become an inheritance of the children of Joseph. (Joshua 24:32)

29. Nazirite or celibacy:

Then the Lord spoke to Moses, saying, ² "Speak to the children of Israel, and say to them: 'When either a man or woman consecrates an offering to take the vow of a Nazirite, to separate himself to the Lord, ³ he shall separate himself from wine and similar drink; he shall drink neither vinegar made from wine nor vinegar made from similar drink; neither shall he drink any grape juice, nor eat fresh grapes or raisins. ⁴ All the days of his separation he shall eat nothing that is produced by the grapevine, from seed to skin. ⁵ All the days of the vow of his separation no razor shall come upon his head; until the days are fulfilled for which he separated himself to the Lord, he shall be holy. Then he shall let the locks of the hair of his head grow. ⁶All the days that he separates himself to the Lord he shall not go near a dead body. ⁷ He shall not make himself unclean even for his father or his mother, for his brother or his sister, when they die, because his separation to God is on his head. ⁸ All the days of his separation he shall be holy to the Lord. ⁹ And if anyone dies very suddenly beside him, and he defiles his consecrated head, then he shall shave his head on the day of his cleansing; on the seventh day he shall shave it. ¹⁰ Then on the eighth day he shall bring two turtledoves or two young pigeons to the priest, to the door of the tabernacle of meeting; ¹¹ and the priest shall offer one as a sin offering and the other as a burnt offering, and make atonement for him, because he sinned in regard to the corpse; and he shall sanctify his head that same day. ¹² He shall consecrate to the Lord the days of his separation, and bring a male lamb in its first year as a trespass offering; but the former days shall be lost because his separation was defiled. ¹³ Now this is the law of the Nazirite: When the days of his separation are fulfilled, he shall be brought to the door of the tabernacle of meeting. ¹⁴ And he shall present his offering to the Lord: one male lamb in its first year without blemish as a burnt offering, one ewe lamb in its first year without blemish as a sin offering, one ram without blemish as a peace offering, ¹⁵ a basket of unleavened bread, cakes of fine flour mixed with oil, unleavened wafers anointed with oil, and their grain offering with their drink offerings. ¹⁶ Then the priest shall bring them before the Lord and offer his sin offering and his burnt offering; ¹⁷ and he shall offer the ram as a sacrifice of a peace offering to the Lord, with the basket of unleavened bread; the priest shall also offer its grain offering and its drink offering. [18] Then the Nazirite shall shave his consecrated head at the door of the tabernacle of meeting, and shall take the hair from his consecrated head and put it on the fire which is under the sacrifice of the peace offering. [19] And the priest shall take the boiled shoulder of the ram, one unleavened cake from the basket, and one unleavened wafer, and put them upon the hands of the Nazirite after he has shaved his consecrated hair, [20] and the priest shall wave them as a wave offering before the Lord; they are holy for the priest, together with the breast of the wave offering and the thigh of the heave offering. After that the Nazirite may drink wine.' [21] "This is the law of the Nazirite who vows to the Lord the offering for his separation, and besides that, whatever else his hand is able to provide; according to the vow which he takes, so he must do according to the law of his separation." [22] And the Lord spoke to Moses, saying: [23] "Speak to Aaron and his sons, saying, 'This is the way you shall bless the children of Israel. Say to them: [24] "The Lord bless you and keep you;[25] The Lord make His face shine upon you, and be gracious to you;[26] The Lord lift up His countenance upon you, and give you peace." ' [27] "So they shall put My name on the children of Israel, and I will bless them." (Numbers 6:1-27)

30. Incense burning custom:

[46] So Moses said to Aaron, "Take a censer and put fire in it from the altar, put incense on it, and take it quickly to the congregation and make atonement for them; for wrath has gone out from the Lord. The plague has begun." [47] Then Aaron took it as Moses commanded, and ran into the midst of the assembly; and already the plague had begun among the people. So he put in the incense and made atonement for the people. [48] And he stood between the dead and the living; so the plague was stopped. [49] Now those who died in the plague were fourteen thousand seven hundred, besides those who died in the Korah incident. [50] So Aaron returned to Moses at the door of the tabernacle of meeting, for the plague had stopped. (Numbers 16:46-50)

31. Sign of Dashain:

And in the seventh month, on the first day of the month, you shall have a holy convocation. You shall do no customary work. For you it is a day of blowing the trumpets. [2] You shall offer a burnt offering as a sweet aroma to the Lord: one young bull, one ram, and seven lambs in their first year, without blemish. [3] Their grain offering shall be fine flour mixed with oil: three-tenths of an ephah for the bull, two-tenths for the ram, [4] and one-tenth for each of the seven lambs; [5] also one kid of the goats as a sin offering, to make atonement for you; [6] besides the burnt offering with its grain offering for the New Moon, the regular burnt offering with its grain offering, and their drink offerings, according to their ordinance, as a sweet aroma, an offering made by fire to the Lord. [7] On the tenth day of this seventh month you shall have a holy convocation. You shall afflict your souls; you shall not do any work. (Numbers 29:1-7). Vijayadashami is a ten day festival.

On the fifteenth day of the seventh month you shall have a holy convocation. You shall do no customary work, and you shall keep a feast to the Lord seven days. (Numbers 29:12). Celebrating seven days indicates Tihar.

32. Witchcraft or soothsayer: *There shall not be found among you anyone who makes his son or his daughter passthrough the fire, or one who practices witchcraft, or a soothsayer, or one who interprets omens, or a sorcerer. (Deuteronomy 18:10)*

33. You shall not muzzle an ox while it treads out the grain. *(Deuteronomy 25:4)*

34. Custom of wearing ephod: *He made the robe of the ephod of woven work, all of blue. (Exodus 39:22)*

35. Burnt offering: *Now the Lord called to Moses, and spoke to him from the tabernacle of meeting. (Leviticus 1:1)*

36. **Grain offering:** *When anyone offers a grain offering to the Lord, his offering shall be of fine flour. And he shall pour oil on it, and put frankincense on it. (Leviticus 2:1)*

37. **Peace offering:** *When his offering is a sacrifice of a peace offering, if he offers it of the herd, whether male or female, he shall offer it without blemish before the Lord. (Leviticus 3:1)*

38. **Sin offering:** *Now the Lord spoke to Moses, saying, [2] "Speak to the children of Israel, saying: 'If a person sins unintentionally against any of the commandments of the Lord in anything which ought not to be done, and does any of them.'" (Leviticus 4:1-2)*

    If a person sins in hearing the utterance of an oath, and is a witness, whether he has seen or known of the matter—if he does not tell it, he bears guilt. (Leviticus 5:1)

39. **Guilt offering:** Then the Lord spoke to Moses, saying: "If a person commits a trespass, and sins unintentionally in regard to the holy things of the Lord, then he shall bring to the Lord as his trespass offering a ram without blemish from the flocks, with your valuation in shekels of silver according to the shekel of the sanctuary, as a trespass offering." (Leviticus 5:14-15)

40. **Burnt Sacrifice:** And the Lord spoke to Moses, saying: "If a person sins and commits a trespass against the Lord by lying to his neighbor about what was delivered to him for safekeeping, or about a pledge, or about a robbery, or if he has extorted from his neighbor." (Leviticus 6:1-2)

41. **Methods of burnt offering:** Then the Lord spoke to Moses, saying, "Command Aaron and his sons, saying, 'This is the law of the burnt offering: The burnt offering shall be on the hearth upon the altar all night until morning, and the fire of the altar shall be kept burning on it.'" (Leviticus 6:8-9)

42. **Grain offering:** This is the law of the grain offering: The sons of Aaron shall offer it on the altar before the Lord. (Leviticus 6:14)

43.Methods of sin offering: [24] Also the Lord spoke to Moses, saying, [25] "Speak to Aaron and to his sons, saying, 'This is the law of the sin offering: In the place where the burnt offering is killed, the sin offering shall be killed before the Lord. It is most holy.'" (Leviticus 6:24-25)

44.Guilt offering:

Likewise, this is the law of the trespass offering (it is most holy): [2] In the place where they kill the burnt offering they shall kill the trespass offering. And its blood he shall sprinkle all around on the altar. [3] And he shall offer from it all its fat. The fat tail and the fat that covers the entrails, [4] the two kidneys and the fat that is on them by the flanks, and the fatty lobe attached to the liver above the kidneys, he shall remove; [5] and the priest shall burn them on the altar as an offering made by fire to the Lord. It is a trespass offering. [6] Every male among the priests may eat it. It shall be eaten in a holy place. It is most holy. [7] The trespass offering is like the sin offering; there is one law for them both: the priest who makes atonement with it shall have it. [8] And the priest who offers anyone's burnt offering, that priest shall have for himself the skin of the burnt offering which he has offered. [9] Also every grain offering that is baked in the oven and all that is prepared in the covered pan, or in a pan, shall be the priest's who offers it. [10] Every grain offering, whether mixed with oil or dry, shall belong to all the sons of Aaron, to one as much as the other. (Leviticus 7:1-10)

45.Don't sacrifice lamb that has any limb too long or too short: Either a bull or a lamb that has any limb too long or too short you may offer as a freewill offering, but for a vow it shall not be accepted. (Leviticus 22:23)

46.Ear piercing: According to Pundit Madhav Prasad Upadhyay's book about ear piercing, the Aryans were servants of the Hebrews. Although it is now fashionable to wear earrings with pierced ears, it means that I am a servant or a slave. Especially the Christians who are the children of the true God means that they are the children of slaves. (Exodus 21:6; 2 Chronicles 33:11; Deuteronomy 15:17)

47. **Prohibition of cooking meat with milk:** The first of the first fruits of your land you shall bring into the house of the Lord your God. You shall not boil a young goat in its mother's milk. (Exodus 23:19)

48. **Do not take bribes:** And you shall take no bribe, for a bribe blinds the discerning and perverts the words of the righteous. (Exodus 23:8)

49. **Levirate marriage:**

If brothers dwell together, and one of them dies and has no son, the widow of the dead man shall not be married to a stranger outside the family; her husband's brother shall go in to her, take her as his wife, and perform the duty of a husband's brother to her. (Deuteronomy 25:5)

This custom is still practiced in different parts of Nepal. **50. Bearing the Ark (Old Testament):**

So, all the work that Solomon had done for the house of the Lord was finished; and Solomon brought in the things which his father David had dedicated: the silver and the gold and all the furnishings. And he put them in the treasuries of the house of God. ²Now Solomon assembled the elders of Israel and all the heads of the tribes, the chief fathers of the children of Israel, in Jerusalem, that they might bring the ark of the covenant of the Lord up from the City of David, which is Zion. ³ Therefore all the men of Israel assembled with the king at the feast, which was in the seventh month. ⁴ So, all the elders of Israel came, and the Levites took up the ark. ⁵ Then they brought up the ark, the tabernacle of meeting, and all the holy furnishings that were in the tabernacle. The priests and the Levites brought them up. ⁶ Also King Solomon, and all the congregation of Israel who were assembled with him before the ark, were sacrificing sheep and oxen that could not be counted or numbered for multitude. [7] Then the priests brought in the ark of the covenant of the Lord to its place, into the inner sanctuary of the temple, to the Most Holy Place, under the wings of the cherubim. [8] For the cherubim spread their wings over the place of the ark, and the cherubim overshadowed the ark and its poles. [9] The poles extended so that the ends of the poles of the ark could be seen from the holy place, in front of the inner sanctuary; but they could not be seen from outside. And they are there to this day. [10] Nothing was in the ark except the two tablets which Moses put there at Horeb, when the Lord made a covenant with the children of Israel, when they had come out of Egypt. [11] And it came to pass when the priests came out of the Most Holy Place (for all the priests who were present had sanctified themselves, without keeping to their divisions), [12] and the Levites who were the singers, all those of Asaph and Heman and Jeduthun, with their sons and their brethren, stood at the east end of the altar, clothed in white linen, having cymbals, stringed instruments and harps, and with them one hundred and twenty priests sounding with trumpets— [13] indeed it came to pass, when the trumpeters and singers were as one, to make one sound to be heard in praising and thanking the Lord, and when they lifted up their voice with the trumpets and cymbals and instruments of music, and praised the Lord, saying: "For He is good, for His mercy endures forever," that the house, the house of the Lord, was filled with a cloud, [14] so that the priests could not continue ministering because of the cloud; for the glory of the Lord filled the house of God. (2 Chronicles 5:1-14)

51. **Hexagon symbol in Nepal:** How did the Jewish flag come to Nepal? How did it come about? Although it cannot be said with certainty, it can be said that this Mongolian community came during the time of the Benei Manasseh because they are ancestor worshipping people. Along with the customs of untouchable communities, there is also a custom of making hexagons by drawing lines in various Mongolian communities. Even in the untouchable community, this custom is still the same. This means that this sign is considered as

an auspicious sign. Now this logo is also used in various universities. The swastika symbol is known as the flag of King David. This trend was already there. Later, after the arrival of the Shah Dynasty king, it is also used by them. This means that it confirms the evidence that Jews were and still are in Nepal.

52. Marchunga: Marchunga is a kind of instrument played by sisters especially in Mongolian society. It started from Israel.

53. Menstruation: If a man lies with a woman during her sickness and uncovers her nakedness, he has exposed her flow, and she has uncovered the flow of her blood. Both of them shall be cut off from their people. (Leviticus 20:18)

Also, you shall not approach a woman to uncover her nakedness as long as she is in her customary impurity. (Leviticus 18:19)

54. The practice of lighting lamps:

Then the Lord spoke to Moses, saying: [2] "Command the children of Israel that they bring to you pure oil of pressed olives for the light, to make the lamps burn continually. [3] Outside the veil of the Testimony, in the tabernacle of meeting, Aaron shall be in charge of it from evening until morning before the Lord continually; it shall be a statute forever in your generations. [4] He shall be in charge of the lamps on the pure gold lampstand before the Lord continually. [5] "And you shall take fine flour and bake twelve cakes with it. Two-tenths of an ephah shall be in each cake. [6] You shall set them in two rows, six in a row, on the pure gold table before the Lord. [7] And you shall put pure frankincense on each row, that it may be on the bread for a memorial, an offering made by fire to the Lord. [8] Every Sabbath he shall set it in order before the Lord continually, being taken from the children of Israel by an everlasting covenant. [9] And it shall be for Aaron and his sons, and they shall eat it in a holy place; for it is most holy to him from the offerings of the Lord made by fire, by a perpetual statute." (Leviticus 24:1-9)

55.Kiranti:

The people of Kirjath Arim, Chephirah, and Beeroth, seven hundred and forty-three. (Ezra 2:25)

Mattaniah, Bakbukiah, Obadiah, Meshullam, Talmon, and Akkub were gatekeepers keeping the watch at the storerooms of the gates. (Nehemiah 12:25)

56.It cannot be said that the Damais are not Jews:

[59] And these were the ones who came up from Tel Melah, Tel Harsha, Cherub, Addan, and Immer; but they could not identify their father's house or their genealogy, whether they were of Israel: [60] the sons of Delaiah, the sons of Tobiah, and the sons of Nekoda, six hundred and fifty-two; [61] and of the sons of the priests: the sons of Habaiah, the sons of Koz, and the sons of Barzillai, who took a wife of the daughters of Barzillai the Gileadite, and was called by their name. [62] These sought their listing among those who were registered by genealogy, but they were not found; therefore, they were excluded from the priesthood as defiled. [63] And the governor said to them that they should not eat of the most holy things till a priest could consult with the Urim and Thummim. (Ezra 2:59-63)

57.Tradition of binding with leather:
In various communities of Nepal, there is a custom of binding leather on the hands of small children. It has a deeper meaning. It is a sign of protection from being touched by any satanic element.

[6] "And these words which I command you today shall be in your heart. [7]You shall teach them diligently to your children, and shall talk of them when you sit in your house, when you walk by the way, when you lie down, and when you rise up. [8]You shall bind them as a sign on your hand, and they shall be as frontlets between your eyes. (Deuteronomy 6:6-8)

58.The custom of putting on Tika:
It shall be as a sign to you on your hand and as a memorial between your eyes, that the Lord's law

may be in your mouth; for with a strong hand the Lord has brought you out of Egypt. (Exodus 13:9)

It shall be as a sign on your hand and as frontlets between your eyes, for by strength of hand the Lord brought us out of Egypt." (Exodus 13:16)

Baal, the Canaanite deity, which resembles the idols of bulls found in Hindu temples. Photo Courtesy: Christianty Today, "Who is Baal in the Bible?"

https://www.christianity.com/wiki/bible/who-is-baal-in-the-bible.html

Gratitude

I am grateful to Rev. Dambar Adhikari.

I express my sincere thanks to him for appreciating my book Revelation of Jesus Christ in Vedanta Philosophy, and recommending the same to the readers.

-Pandit Madhav Upadhyaya,

February 13, 2021,

Champasari Pradhannagar,

Pin 734003 Siliguri- Dist. Darjeeling W. B. India

Conclusion

This book has attempted to make clear the solid proof that our Mongolian community is of Jewish origin and the children of Benei Manasseh are not any lowly and unholy community. They are not untouchable community, but instead, in His mercy, for thousands of years, God has prevented them from worshiping the handiwork of men. Abundant evidence has been given that the Benei Ephraim and Benei Israel are the descendants of the Levites.

According to a deep study of the crown and the throne of the King of Egypt and background of our Shah Dynasty community, the throne of the Pharaoh King has a bull snake and the head of a cobra is also seen on the crown. This means that the Shah Dynasty kings are descendants of the Egyptian Ishmael. The Aryans have been worshiping Hitler's swastika, though turning it upside down. It also has a deep meaning. This sign is considered a very dangerous sign in Europe. They are ill-disposed to the Christians, the Dalits, and the Mongols- the people of God. In fact, it is God who is the creator of these four communities and Noah's descendants came to Nepal after migrating from their sons, which is confirmed by archaeological and biblical accounts, as well as from the striking similarities of the festivals and musical instruments found in these communities.

In the end, this book is written as an attempt to shed light on this hidden and mysterious truth.

'What agreement is there between the temple of God and idols? For we are the temple of the living God. As God has said: "I will live with them and walk among them, and I will be their God, and they will be my people." Therefore, "Come out from them and be separate, says the

Lord. Touch no unclean thing, and I will receive you." And, "I will be a Father to you, and you will be my sons and daughters, says the Lord Almighty'" (2 Corinthians 6:16-18).

It is my prayer that all the oppressed and suppressed communities come to know this truth and be set free. And we all humanity may live in harmony and peace, glorifying our Creator God, whom we have the privilege of addressing as our Abba, Father. Only the Lord Jesus Christ, the God-Man, can redeem us; only in Him can we find forgiveness and healing.

May the Lord bless us all.

Thank you!

References

Balakumari. *Bible Journey.* Pps. 162-163.

Daniel, Glyn Edmund. "archaeology". *Encyclopedia Britannica,* 15 Sep. 2022, <https:// www.britannica.com/science/archaeology>. Accessed 1 January 2023. Jews of India - Bene Israel

Jewish Virtual Libarary, (*Marks and Israel* Sieff)

Jewish Virtual Library. Tailoring. Talmud.

<http://www.Jewishvirtuallibrary.org>. Accessed 29/12/2022. source/judaica/ejud_0002_0001. Wikipedia, the free encyclopedia. http://en.wikipedia.org/wiki/kami (page 4 from 21)

Khanal, Dr. BP. *Prithak Bichar* (Uncommon Thoughts). Page 282. Mukarung, Shrawan. "BISE NAGARCHI KO BAYAN." February 24.2014/ shrawan Mukarung

Mukarung We're all Bise Nagarchis- Nepali Times

Marandy, Rosemary. "Living in the Shadow of Rebellion: India's Gond Tribe" (750 Gond Clans; Madhya Pradesh 5,093,123; Odisha 888,581; Bihar 256,738; Maharasthra 1,618,090)

< https://pulitzercenter.org/stories/living-shadow-rebellion-indias-gond tribe>

Raunakms. "Genetic Ancestry of Nepalis".

https://raunakms.wordpress.com/2012/05/14/genetic-ancestry-of-nepalis/. Accessed 28/12/2022.

Riva MA, Belingheri M, De Vito G, Lucchini R. Bernardino Ramazzini (1633-1714). J Neurol. 2018 Sep;265(9):2164-2165. doi: 10.1007/

s00415-018-8733-y. Epub 2018 Jan 11. PMID: 29327285; PMCID: PMC6057829.<https://www.ncbi.nlm.nih.gov/pmc/articles/PMC6057829/>. Accessed 29/12/2022.

Sefaria Edition 2021, Translated by Rabbi Francis Nataf. <https://www.sefaria.org/ Sefer_HaMitzvot %2C_Positive_Commandments.1.1?lang=bi&with= About&lang2=en>. Accessed 01/01/2023.

Shalom.<Https://ccnmtl.columbia.edu/projects/mmt/mxp/notes/5140.html#:~:text=%3C,within%20worship%20and%20other%20contexts.

Accessed 01/01/2023.

Sharma, Dr. Bal Krishna. *The origin of caste system in Hinduism and its relevance in the present context.* P.107.

Subba Paul, Chhatra. *Important Names of God.* P. 257.

The South - Asian Page 4 of 6

Yulia Egorova & Shahid Perwez (2012) "Old Memories, New Histories: (Re) discovering the Past of Jewish Dalits, History and Anthropology," 23:1, 1-15, DOI: 10.1080/02757206.2012.649272

Washington Times, the. Jews of India – Bene Israel, Nissim Ezekiel. 2006.

www.ingramcontent.com/pod-product-compliance
Lightning Source LLC
Chambersburg PA
CBHW031550150726
47990CB00001B/285